Judging justice

FEB 21

DATE DUE

Judging justice

An introduction to contemporary political philosophy

Philip Pettit

Professor of Philosophy
University of Bradford

Routledge & Kegan Paul
London, Boston and Henley

First published in 1980
by Routledge & Kegan Paul Ltd
39 Store Street,
London WC1E 7DD,
9 Park Street,
Boston, Mass. 02108, USA and
Broadway House,
Newtown Road,
Henley-on-Thames,
Oxon RG9 1EN

Set in Times Roman by
Input Typesetting Ltd, London
and printed in Great Britain by
Billing & Sons Ltd,
Guildford, London, Oxford and Worcester

© Philip Pettit 1980

British Library Cataloguing in Publication Data

Pettit, Philip

Judging justice.
1. Social justice
I. Title
323.4   HM216   79-42650

ISBN 0 7100 0563 6
ISBN 0 7100 0571 7 Pbk

For Eileen

Contents

Introduction

'If I don't write the book, someone else will.' That thought combined with diffidence to prevent me from publishing the following text some years ago. This year the chemistry of the effect was reversed, when I received encouragement from a colleague who had done me the service of reading through a typescript version. The thought which had earlier inhibited effort, now served to stimulate it. My first duty in introducing the work is to record my gratitude to that colleague, Roger Fellows. May he not be embarrassed by the offspring of his eloquence. Nor, for that matter, may I.

The book is an attempt to bring within a single focus the main lines of thinking in the recent welter of speculation on social justice. This speculation has encompassed the thought of economists such as Kenneth Arrow and Amartya Sen, writers in jurisprudence like H. L. A. Hart and Ronald Dworkin, and philosophers such as John Rawls and Robert Nozick. A philosopher myself, I have been captivated by the confidence and vigour with which these thinkers have re-opened issues in the evaluation of social order that have lain dormant since the heyday of nineteenth-century utilitarianism. They have brought reason again to bear on matters of political assessment, where throughout most of this century questions of value, in contrast to supposedly independent questions of fact, have been consigned to the rationally inscrutable realms of intuition, decision, and feeling.

The text is a moderately original response to this material, assembling and isolating the topics in a slightly distinctive, but I hope not idiosyncratic, way. It explores the three accounts of social justice which have dominated the recent debate. They are: the proprietarian account, which makes natural rights the last court of appeal in political assessment, the utilitarian, which looks to human happiness in the judgment of rival social schemes, and

Introduction

the contractarian, an approach which identifies the just arrangement as that which people would have reason to choose, were
they ignorant of how they would fare under the different alternatives. The first assimilates justice to legitimacy, the second to
welfare, and the third to fairness. The doctrines will not be unfa-
miliar, although 'proprietarianism' is a novel piece of nomencla-
ture. The term is manufactured from 'propriety', a synonym of
legitimacy, and if it smacks of 'property' and 'proprietor', that can
be tolerated too: the theory is notoriously associated with respect
for the claims of ownership.

These three theories of justice have all had classical incarnations
but the book is mainly concerned with their contemporary representatives. Proprietarianism is considered almost exclusively in
the light of Robert Nozick's *Anarchy, State and Utopia*, Blackwell,
Oxford, 1974. Utilitarianism, while it is discussed by reference to
Bentham and Mill, is given an interpretation in the terms of
contemporary utility theory. And contractarianism, as is hardly
surprising, is represented as the doctrine canonically formulated
in John Rawls's *A Theory of Justice*, Oxford University Press,
1972. In each case I examine the criterion of justice advanced by
the doctrine; I consider the consequence of applying that criterion
in practice; and finally I look into the question of how vulnerable
the theory is to criticism. Each doctrine receives attention in a
section of three chapters, and the three tasks mentioned are div-
ided out among those chapters.

It will not escape notice that these three attempts to justify the
demands of justice come from a common background. They suppose a shared account of the task of political philosophy, and a
version of this is elaborated in Part I. More significantly, however,
the doctrines all assume that social institutions are perfectible and
that their purpose is to serve the interests of individuals; in a
distinctive sense, they are all individualistic theories of justice.
The underlying individualism is dissected and defended in Part II
of the book. Until someone is persuaded that an individualistic
view of the relation between individuals and institutions is justified, he can have no interest in the theories of justice examined
here. The individualism in question, it should be noticed, is a
rather more modest doctrine than many views which have borne
that name: the point is made clear in the text.

It is common to find individualistic theories of justice pilloried
as liberal fantasies. What is less common is a recognition of the
restricted alternatives to the elaboration of an individualistic theory. One may adopt the stance, common to certain revolutionaries
and reactionaries, that there is no judging the worth of institutional arrangements, a viewpoint which makes people into spec-

tators of or collaborators in the historical process. Or one may go for the slightly more palatable outlook developed recently by Jürgen Habermas. According to this theory, which I discuss briefly in chapter 3, one can hold that the just social order is that which would be selected by people negotiating under circumstances of undistorted relationships, without believing that there is a method presently available for identifying that order. I characterise the theory as consensualism, because it represents the just dispensation as that which would command rational consensus under ideal conditions of bargaining.

Recourse to consensualism, or to any such sceptical view, should be a last resort. Before espousing it, one should have been given powerful reasons for distrusting individualistic attempts to specify the demands of justice, or one should have proved for oneself that those attempts are failures. In my opinion, there are no reasons in principle for suspecting the individualistic enterprise, although there are many obstacles to clear perception and argument, obstacles well documented in the literature on ideology and false consciousness. If one is to opt for consensualism or the like, I think that it should be after exploring the plausibility of an individualistic construal of justice. Thus there is no reason why someone of a Marxist persuasion, for example, should think the effort intellectually beneath him, even if it is an enterprise to which Marx himself gave regrettably little attention. I should mention that my own attitude to the individualistic theories of justice discussed in this text is an exploratory one. Where the discussion leads is a matter best postponed until the conclusion, but I can say that at the end of it I retain a healthy respect for the consensualist position.

There are a number of different sorts of questions relevant to political thinking and it will be useful to be clear on which we are raising. Our concern is with the specification of the just social order, a task characterised in the first part of the text. This is a traditional philosophical concern and it should be distinguished from two closely related ones. To describe and disavow these at once, we are interested neither in the scientific question of what social orders can arise from the existing one, nor in the practical question of what we are obliged to do by way of transforming the existing order into a more just dispensation. Political philosophy in the sense in which it is here discussed is an abstract, even a rarefied, discipline, being focused on the ideal structure of society. Thus it ignores such practical issues as the following: 'How far should I comply with a relatively unjust *status quo*?', 'How heavily should I weigh the duty of civic compliance against other obligations?', 'What efforts should I make, in particular what illegal efforts, to alter the existing order?', 'If the order is changed, to what extent should existing claims be recognised in the realloca- tion of goods?' But although it is abstract, the discipline is import- ant. For if one cannot say how society should be organised in an ideal world, how can one know what changes should be wrought in its mundane equivalent?

Like the curate's egg, the text undoubtedly has its better parts and its worse. What is even more certain is that it has its straight- forward stretches, and its bumpy ones. The first chapter may be found relatively hard going and a cursory reading can be recom- mended to the timid of heart: this should be enough for an under- standing of what follows. The toughest philosophical chapter is probably chapter 6 and, so long as the reader knows what is argued there, it can be skipped without great loss. The most technical chapter is chapter 12, which deals with putting the util- itarian criterion into practice, and this can also be omitted without serious deprivation. The text should be intelligible to anyone who can tolerate a little abstraction, though it will require effort in the non-professional reader. It is designed in particular to be acces- sible to the undergraduate student, at least in the context of background tutorial work. There is a summary at the end of each chapter, and also a short guide to relevant reading.

The text originated as a set of lectures at University College, Dublin in 1975–6. Before that the material was worked up for teaching purposes at Trinity Hall, Cambridge and since then it has served me in presenting courses at the University of Bradford. Many of my students have given me help: in criticism, in encour- agement and, it must be admitted, in incomprehension. I thank them one and all. I also owe a debt of gratitude to the numerous colleagues and friends with whom I have discussed questions in the text. I must mention in particular Chris Hookway, Joel Kup- perman, John Maguire, Fred Schick, Richard Tuck, Denys Turner, and my philosophical colleagues at Bradford: Roger Fel- lows, Gregory des Jardins, Richard Lindley and Graham Mac- donald. Two research students who have goaded and pressed me into making something better of my argument are Chris Bonning- ton and David West. My thanks to them too. And finally, my thanks to Verna Wadelin, who make light work of typing the manuscript, and to Denise Martin who helped in the assembly of the bibliography.

Part I Philosophy, politics and society

1 *Social life*

In order to get our discussion going we need to develop a picture of what social life involves. Political evaluation, the central theme of our considerations, has to do with the proper ordering of social life and we must give ourselves an image of the matter that is to be ordered. The picture that will be presented has, it should be stressed, only descriptive pretensions. It picks out salient features in the landscape of society but it does so without implying that other distributions of emphasis are impossible or that the features highlighted are important for their causal efficacy. The value of the representation is that it gives us terms of reference, terms in which to formulate and explore the problems which concern us, and it can have that value without serving every expressive and explanatory purpose in relation to the matter represented.

The first thing to be said about social life, and it makes the initial bold stroke on our canvas, is that anything which counts as a significant social event can be characterised by reference to individuals. This comes of the fact that individuals are the entities out of which society is constituted and that, just as a whole does or suffers nothing that is not done or suffered by its parts, so society undergoes no visitation and sustains no activity that is not undergone or sustained by individual people. But what, it may be asked, of a natural catastrophe: is this not a significant social event, although it is not something that intrinsically involves individuals? The answer, I suggest, is that the event has social significance only in so far as it bears other descriptions that refer us to individuals, such as a description of it as affecting people's fortunes, opportunities, or attitudes. The cosmic ray that passes through the atmosphere, unnoticed and innocuous, is not a social event, and neither would any happening be that failed of a connection with persons.

Even with this first stroke we must be careful to enter qualifications, for otherwise the proposition will be found unnecessarily contentious. Specifically, we must disavow any expressive exhaustiveness or explanatory adequacy that we might be thought to be claiming for the proposition. On the first point: it is not suggested that social life cannot also be represented as the systematic fulfilment of certain roles, as the reliable reproduction of certain structures, or whatever. And on the second: it is not implied that the causal explanation of patterns in social life must refer us ultimately to the autonomous agency of people; what are parts of a whole may also be its pawns. In Part II below we shall defend a view that confers a certain causal ultimacy on individual agents, but even someone who attacked that depiction of things would have to accept the proposition under discussion now.

The second thing to be said in description of social life, and it is no less a platitude than the first, is that people form groups of a smaller scale than society itself and that much of what they do and suffer in social life entails the doing or suffering of groups. That people form such alliances is indisputable, for no one will deny the reality of families and villages, gangs and clubs, unions and associations, companies and institutes, or even nations and classes. That these groups are implicated in the fortunes of the individuals who compose them can be borne out by example. The actions of individuals can mean that something is done or undergone by a group of which they are members: if they complain in the group's name, then the group complains too; if they quarrel among themselves then the group suffers the consequence, experiencing crisis or perhaps breaking up. And the things passively borne by individuals can also entail that there is something done or undergone by a group they form: if they each succumb to an appropriate rule of law, this can mean that the group achieves identity or cohesion; if they are each wiped out then, unless it is a case where others can claim to carry it on, the group will be wiped out too.

Groups are important in social life because they can be agents in their own right. A group is not just a collection of individuals, for it can remain one and the same through a change of membership. A family does not become a different entity through the birth or death of a child, a company does not mutate in the turnover of its directors, a nation does not lose its identity as one generation replaces another. Each such group collects individuals together at any time but it does so in the manner of a collective rather than a collection. The collective is distinguished from the collection by the fact that though it may at any time have the same members as some collections it is conceptualised differently. A change that would mark a change of identity in the collection,

2

one set of items giving way to another, can pass as an accidental alteration in the collective. The collective is seen on the model of a physical object, its members at any time corresponding to the parts of the object and its continuing identity being no more dependent on sameness of members than is that of the object on sameness of parts.

As a collective, a group may have interests which its members, or at least those of its members in certain representative positions, are committed to pursuing, regardless of their personal feelings. Thus it may act so as to make commitments which are credible independently of the personal attitudes of its representatives. And, making such commitments, it can incur obligations and enjoy rights over and beyond those that accrue to its members. In these regards groups, especially formally organised groups such as companies and institutes, mimic individual agents. All that is done in social life may be the responsibility of individuals but their agency is sometimes exercised in their own name and sometimes in the name of those other agents that they help to constitute. The bank clerk who cashes your cheque, the city hall secretary who sends the rates bill, the tax official who scrutinises your return of income: these are agents in whom mentality and temperament have been temporarily replaced by official commission; they do not act in their own names, but rather corporate agents act through them.

On the picture as it has been sketched in so far, social life is at bottom the life of individual agents, but these agents form groups and groups can themselves have the character of agents. Before we add a third element to the picture, a remark on the formation of groups may be in place. Whether a collection of people is to be regarded as a group depends on how significantly distinctive is the way they treat one another and the way they treat, and are treated by, outsiders. It also sometimes depends on how self-conscious people are of belonging to the collection: because of lack of self-consciousness we might want to say that the collection of people over seven feet tall do not form a group, even though they may satisfy the first requirement. Because of the variety of groups it is difficult to formulate more exactly general conditions necessary for a collection to count as a group. Families and nations, clubs and institutes, each have contrasting features that are as salient as what they have in common. And a further source of complexity is that historical circumstance has an important influence on group formation. Feudal life, for example, did not require, and therefore did not encourage, the emergence of the limited liability company which became the hallmark of nineteenth-century capitalism. In order to parse a society into groups one would need a sense of the circumstances prevailing and the purposes which people are liable to want served.

Now for the third, and final, contribution to our canvas of social life. There are three gross aspects to the behaviour of people in society, whether they are behaving in their own name or in the name of a group, and these give us three major divisions in social life. The areas are distinguished from one another by characteristic regularities of behaviour and by the result which those regularities bring about in each case. I dub them respectively the civil, the economic and the legal parts of social life. The civil is marked by the regular treatment which individuals and groups mete out to one another in virtue of which they are constituted, in the most basic social sense, as persons. The economic is identified by the regular treatment that leads us to describe some persons as the owners of certain things. And the legal is demarcated by the regular treatment which establishes some persons as authorities in certain matters.

We must make a brief digression about the sort of regularity involved in each of these cases. What is required is not just that nearly everyone behaves in the manner in question, under the appropriate circumstances. Such behaviour might come about through the accident of similar motivation, or whatever, and it is not accidental that individuals and groups generally conform to civil, economic and legal regularities. Suppose that people all peel potatoes in the same way, drawing the knife towards them and raising the trajectory near the end of the movement. There is more than a regularity of this kind involved in the behaviour whereby content is given to the notion of the person, or the owner, or the authority. One feature missing in the potato-peeling case is knowledge on the part of each person who conforms to the regularity that nearly every other person conforms too: such knowledge may be present but again it may not. By contrast we shall see that it is scarcely possible to imagine an institutional regularity of the kind that we are discussing which is not a matter of common knowledge, i.e. such that not only does nearly everyone conform, but nearly everyone also expects nearly everyone else to conform too.

But let us imagine that everyone peels potatoes in the same way, and further that everyone knows that this is so. Does general knowledge plus general conformity make the regularity indistinguishable from our civil, economic and legal regularities? I think not, for the reason that there is no connection hypothesised between the obtaining of the conformity and the presence of the knowledge. If someone ceased to know that nearly everyone peeled potatoes as he does, this would hardly affect his own way of peeling them; thus we could expect the regularity to continue to be observed, even in the absence of knowledge that it is generally respected. By contrast it seems in the case of the institutional regularity that there is at least a weak motivational link between an individual's expectation of general conformity and his tendency to conform himself. The link may not be indispensable, in the sense that the person would conform even if it were not there; and it may also be unconstraining, in the sense that it may allow him on occasion not to conform. One is tempted to formulate it by saying that the individual's awareness that conformity is general gives him some reason to conform himself, but that will not do either because in the cases where free-riding is attractive the awareness may have the contrary effect: knowledge that nearly everyone else will conform to the civil regularity of contributing to emergency needs may give me reason not to contribute myself, assuring me that such needs will be met without my help. The formulation to which one is driven is something like the following: that the individual's awareness that conformity is general gives him some reason to want deviance discouraged, including his own deviance if that is the cost of general discouragement. The idea is that the regularity is of such a kind that the individual's awareness that it is generally observed gives him some reason to want it protected against deviance, the state of affairs liable to result from deviance being less attractive than general conformity to the regularity. We shall come to understand the idea better when we look later at some illustrative examples.

We have formulated three conditions which any regularity in civil, economic or legal life must fulfil, at least if it is to be effective in the constitution of personhood, ownership or authority. The argument for the conditions is inseparable from the case for our analysis as a whole. The conditions describe a species of regularity, which I shall call a practice, and it is reasonable to impose them if, with the help of this category, we can present an empirically supportable and theoretically unified analysis of the major areas of social life. Whether our analysis is all of that should appear shortly, and will be left to the judgment of the reader. For the moment it will suffice to present the conditions as part of a stipulative definition, the rightness or wrongness of which does not arise. To restate those conditions for convenience of reference, although without all the precision a formal definition would require, a regularity of behaviour is a practice in a given society only if:

1 nearly everyone conforms to it;
2 nearly everyone expects nearly everyone else to conform;
3 this expectation gives nearly everyone some reason for wanting

deviance discouraged, including his own deviance if that is a necessary cost of general discouragement.

Let us go back now to the different divisions we have identified in social life. The regularities, more strictly the practices, that mark off civil life are a relatively open class which exemplify generic categories like the following: non-violence, non-fraudulence, truth-telling, promise-keeping, and benevolence. General conformity to such regularities, or at least to a subset of them, would appear to be a precondition of society: in a world without it life, in Hobbes's phrase, would be solitary, poor, nasty, brutish and short. It is not a happy accident of social existence, but an essential feature of it, that people are generally non-violent, honest, truthful, reliable and kind, or, to mention some culturally specific variations of these categories, that they make sound colleagues, faithful spouses, and good friends. The civil life constituted by conformity to these regularities is the base on which the other strata of society rest.

Conformity to the regularities is forthcoming as a matter of practice rather than fortuitously. In society people do not just conform themselves; they expect others mostly to conform; and this being so they have some reason to want deviance to be discouraged. That the first two conditions are fulfilled is empirically irresistible and that the last is so follows from the fact that the discouragement of deviance serves at least a double purpose: it preserves the regularity from the possible erosive effects of trespass and, even if that is not thought to be necessary, it protects each party from the injury that a deviant may inflict, even as it prevents each party from inflicting injury. But our definition of a practice has it that the reason which people have to want deviance discouraged turns on their expecting others generally to conform: this is the crucial motivational link between expectation and acceptance that distinguishes practices. Is the feature borne out by civil regularities? Yes, for a number of reasons. There is no regularity to be preserved unless others generally conform, and it may not seem likely that discouragement of deviance would bring about the regularity *ex nihilo*. Besides, in a state of civil anarchy one might have little reason for wanting violence, fraud and so on discouraged, for one might well fear the uncertain effects of such interference with the *status quo*: it could harm one more than it helps.

It is important that the regularities of civil life are forthcoming as a matter of practice, for it is this which assures each individual or group that it is possible to rely on the support of others in the event of obstruction or injury from another. If everyone has a reason to want deviance to be discouraged in respect of some regularity then in normal circumstances anyone who is criticised for conformity, or injured through nonconformity, can expect at least the minimal support of having his opponent put in the wrong, while he is represented as blameless. Even if a formal system of discouragement is not instituted, with tribunals and sanctions and so on, it must be expected of people who sustain a practice that they will give it their moral support, calling criticism down on those who deviate and even perhaps ostracising them. For the regularities of civil life to gain the confidence of parties in society, it is necessary that they can rely on support of this kind. Otherwise they must face the risk of being isolated in confrontation with deviants.

Civil practices are each of them ways of dispensing a single commodity: respect. This word sums up all that is bestowed on someone as he is made the beneficiary of non-violence, non-fraudulence, truth-telling, promise-keeping and benevolence. On the other side, to be the beneficiary of such treatment, to count as an appropriate object of respect, is in a social, if not a metaphysical, sense of the term, to be a person. The sense of being a person which is in question here is that supposed when we say that Jews were non-persons in Nazi Germany, or that a child or lunatic is a full person of society through the intermediacy of a guardian or trustee. To be a person in this sense is, we can say, to be an accepted party to the civil practices of the society. It is to be locked into the system of mutual expectation which leads one to anticipate respect from others and to offer them respect in return. It is to have grounds for complaint when respect is denied by others, and to give grounds for complaint when one denies respect oneself: to be recognised within the society at once as a party deserving and as a party responsible.

The parties which become persons through their engagement in civil practices include groups as well as individuals. It is always individuals who act, as we have seen, but they may act in an individual or an institutional capacity and in the latter case we can perfectly sensibly speak of groups acting through them. Thus there is no problem with the idea that groups can give respect. And neither is there a problem with the idea of their receiving respect in return. It may not make sense with every sort of group to think of exercising benevolence or even non-violence towards it, but it will always be in place to practise truth-telling, promise-keeping and non-fraudulence. We must not be surprised then if a group is given the status of a person in our society, albeit that of a juristic rather than a natural person. The classic example of the juristic person is the limited liability company, but a great variety of groups, especially formally organised ones, have this standing in law.

The practices of economic life confer on some of the persons recognised in civil practices the extra distinction of being owners; if they accord this to individuals or groups which are less than full persons, that is exceptional. Like personhood, in the sense in which we have spoken of it, ownership is not something that exists prior to the organisation of social life. Clearly for example it is not a physically definable relationship between a person and the thing owned: it does not consist in bodily possession, and need not even entail it. Rather, just as to be a person is to have the moral support of others in resisting a certain sort of irregular criticism or injury, so to own something is to have their moral support against complaint about employing it in a certain manner or against obstruction to that employment of it. Ownership is an essentially social phenomenon.

To recognise the social nature of ownership is to be referred to practices which underlie it, in parallel to the practices underlying personhood. The most economical, and empirically the most plausible, explanation of how one can invoke moral support against complaint or interference is that in using the object owned in the fashion in question one is conforming to a practice of the society, whereas the person who obstructs one using it in that way is offending against that practice. A practice is a regularity to which nearly everyone conforms, to which nearly everyone expects that others will generally conform, and which nearly everyone has some reason, granted that expectation, to want protected against deviance. If one's employment of the thing in question is in conformity with such a practice then in normal circumstances one may expect people generally to discourage deviance, at least to the extent of holding one blameless and calling down criticism on anyone who interferes with that employment of the object.

The practices in the background of ownership, assuming that there are such, establish two things: first, the various conditions under which one may expect moral support for using an object appropriately or resisting interference with that use; and second, the manner of use which one may hope to be regarded as appropriate and worthy of support. The conditions give the titles to ownership, the manner of use its rights. The main titles to ownership in contemporary western society are given by: production in self-employment; production with the help of employees; exchange and purchase; endowment and inheritance; and, in the case of animals, procreation by a female in one's ownership already. The rights which go with these titles vary greatly with the sort of property in question. One may do with one's car lots of things that one may not do with one's house, and with one's house a variety of things one would be forbidden to do with one's cat. Where one may take the car to pieces, one will probably not be allowed to demolish the house. And where one may paint the house, at least on the inside, it is doubtful in the present day whether one would be allowed to paint the cat.

Is it empirically plausible, as claimed, to describe these regularities whereby persons suffer one another to keep a certain hold on certain things as practices? Unlike the respect which constitutes persons, this sufferance may not seem to be dispensed in the ready manner we might expect in a practice. After all in giving respect one may anticipate like in return, but for giving sufferance one may be granted precious little: one may be a pauper. Give or take a qualification, persons are equally persons, but there is no sense in which they are equally owners, at least not in an inegalitarian society.

This point is an important one, and must be incorporated in our understanding of ownership, but it does not mean that we cannot speak of practices of sufferance. The economic regularities of a society attract general conformity, they are expected by nearly everyone to attract the general conformity of others, and, at least in the absence of plausible alternative regularities, this expectation gives nearly everyone some reason to want to have deviance from the regularities discouraged. The last clause is the crucial one, for it may be wondered why someone would want to have a property dispensation preserved by sanction whose effect is to impoverish him. The answer to the puzzle, and the reason why even a massively impoverishing regularity can pass for a practice, is contained in the phrase: in the absence of plausible alternative regularities. An economic regimen which makes one poor, and which one regards as inferior to many alternatives, may yet be better than economic chaos. And the expectation that others will generally conform to the existing set of regularities may make chaos seem the only alternative. Thus it may give one some reason why one should want deviance to be discouraged, including one's own deviance if that is a cost of restraining others. Notice though that the reason given may, of course, be outweighed by all sorts of other reasons, from the ethical to the egoistic, for wanting the deviance to go ahead. And notice too that the reason given may not make just any sort of discouragement seem desirable. All that is required is the weakest form of motivational link between the expectation that others will conform and one's acquiescence in the regularity: it is this which marks off a practice from an accidental regularity of which one happens to be aware, such as the potato-peeling example that we imagined.

Despite all of these qualifications, someone may object that it is misleading to speak of practices of economic sufferance, with the implications of consent which that way of speaking carries, in those situations where many people are pauperised. At the limit I must agree. There can be exploitation in a society where economic regularities come by way of practice, for the regularities may have an appeal to many only because of the unavailability of better alternatives; what exploitation often means indeed is persuading people towards a course that puts them at a relative disadvantage by pointing out that alternative courses are even less appealing. But when a situation comes about in which it is only the immediate threat of force that keeps most of the people in line with the economic regularities I am prepared to agree that it is misleading to speak of practices. Here the link is broken between expectation of conformity by others and acceptance of the regularities to which they conform. We do not find any longer something that is properly a form of social life, but the brute phenomenon of psychological and physical control. Fortunately, however, such situations are comparatively rare and, that being so, we can regard the economic regimen described in our model of practices as at least the normal case.

Where civil practices constitute persons, and economic practices owners, what I call legal practices establish authorities: these are persons, individual or institutional, who have a special decision-making role on public matters. In social life the major authorities on public matters are, in the traditional terminology, the legislative, judicial and executive organs of the state. The legislature, in the form of the Houses of Parliament, Congress, or whatever, spells out some of the existing civil and economic practices as laws of the land, and supports them with sanctions; also it introduces new laws to supplement, and sometimes to subvert, existing practices. The judiciary, comprising all the courts in the country, makes decisions on whether the laws have been trespassed in given cases, interpreting hitherto vague laws in the process, and imposes sanctions where it judges that they have. The executive, which encompasses the Government, Civil Service, Police Force, and so on, is meant to serve the legislature and judiciary, promulgating and applying the laws, bringing offenders before the courts, and carrying out the sanctions imposed. It does this, although in modern societies it also does much more, usually exercising significant control for example on what goes before the legislature, and even holding sway over legislative decisions through the influence of the party machine. In the next chapter we shall see something of the further reaches of power to which the executive aspires, but they can pass here without comment.

Just as owning something is not a matter of physical possession, so having authority does not come down to brute force. If an individual or group has authority in a certain matter, that means that its decision will be generally accepted, but not just because the individual or group brooks no opposition. It must be, as in the economic case, and indeed also the civil one, that the body has the moral support of most of the society against complaint about its taking a decision in the matter, if not about the decision taken, and against interference with its decision-making activity. Authority, unlike brute power, is an essentially social matter.

Again in parallel to the economic case, we can argue here that the social nature of authority refers us to practices which underlie the phenomenon. The best explanation of how an authority can invoke moral support against those who criticise or obstruct it is that in taking a decision in the public matter in question the authority is conforming to a practice of the society, whereas the person who obstructs it is offending against that practice. Suppose that there is a regularity whereby nearly everyone accepts the decision of a certain body in a certain matter, expects nearly everyone else to accept it, and is given some reason by that expectation to want any deviation from the regularity to be discouraged. In that event it is understandable why nearly everyone should support the body against irregular complaint or interference, at least to the extent of holding the opponent out of order.

Economic practices, we saw, establish titles and rights in respect of ownership. Similarly legal practices define the titles and rights of authority. Political regimes are distinguished by the nature of these definitions. In a democracy like the United Kingdom, the title to legislative authority, at least for the House of Commons, comes from popular election, the title to executive authority, so far as the Government is concerned, from control over the House of Commons, and the title to judicial authority from appointment by the Government. The rights of each authority are determined by law and tradition, albeit a particularly hallowed tradition, in the United Kingdom, and in many other countries by a written constitution, supplemented by particular laws. One of the constraints on the rights of government that has traditionally been regarded as distinctive of democracy is that it may not interfere with the decisions of the judiciary. Many other such constraints exist but it would be boring to spell them out.

Where civil practices dispense respect to persons and economic practices sufferance to owners, legal practices give authorities recognition. Unlike respect, however, recognition parallels sufferance in being almost inevitably distributed in an unequal pattern: persons may be equally persons, but they are almost never

11

equally owners or authorities. Does the fact of such inequality make it unrealistic to speak of authority being established by practices? No, except as in the economic case, at the very limit of the imposition of power. Up to that point, and even in situations where we would unhesitantly speak of tyranny, it may plausibly be the case not only that nearly everyone conforms to the regularities of recognition and that nearly everyone expects others generally to conform, but that this expectation gives nearly everyone some reason to want deviance from the regularities discouraged. The reason is that there may be no viable alternative to the existing order other than chaos. Notice here again, however, that the connection postulated between expectation and acquiescence, the connection that distinguishes practices, is very weak indeed: nearly everyone is given some reason to want discouragement of deviance, but that reason may be balanced by other reasons for wanting deviance to go ahead, and it need not be a reason for wanting just any sort of discouragement, such as police terror and intimidation.

In this chapter we have given ourselves a useful image of what social life involves. We have seen that, at bottom, the subjects of social life are individual agents; that these individuals form various groups, and that such groups can take on the character of institutional agents; and that the three major aspects to the social life enjoyed by both these sorts of agents are the civil, the economic and the legal. The civil is distinguished by practices that constitute the persons of society, the economic by practices that establish the owners, and the legal by practices that institute the authorities. The practices in question in each case are regularities of behaviour to which nearly everyone conforms, whether acting in an individual or institutional capacity, to which nearly everyone expects others generally to conform, and in which nearly everyone is motivated by that expectation to acquiesce: specifically, nearly everyone is given some reason by the expectation to want deviance from the regularity discouraged. With this picture of social life fixed in our minds we can now turn to consider the nature and variety of political issues.

Bibliographical note

The emergence of group agents in social life is nicely treated, both analytically and historically, in James S. Coleman, *Power and the Structure of Society*, Norton, New York, 1974. The approach to social life which emphasises regularities or rules of behaviour stems from the classic recent text in the philosophy of law, H. L. A. Hart, *The Concept of Law*, Oxford University Press 1961. This approach is usefully discussed by someone who criticises Hart in some of the uses he makes of it: Ronald Dworkin, *Taking Rights Seriously*, Duckworth, London, 1978, chapters 2 and 3. The treatment of the concept of a practice in the text is heavily influenced by the definition of conventional regularities, a species of practice, in David Lewis, *Convention*, Harvard University Press, 1969. A recent extended discussion of related issues is Edna Ullman-Margalit, *The Emergence of Norms*, Oxford University Press, 1977. There is a fuller account of groups and practices in Graham Macdonald and Philip Pettit, *Semantics and Social Science*, Routledge & Kegan Paul, London, forthcoming, chapter 3.

2   Political issues

The picture of social life developed in the last chapter is put to use in this, for it enables us to set out a nice account of the different sorts of issues that come up in politics. Politics may be taken here as the activity of arranging the legal practices of a society *vis-à-vis* its civil and economic ones. It is conceivable that a society should emerge and take shape through such a gradual and accommodating process that we would hesitate to say that political activity had any part in its appearance. What is extremely unlikely, however, is that politics should not come on the scene at any stage. Inevitably, as the authorities of the clan or tribe or nation get established, even where they are the informal, unforceful bodies envisaged by political minimalists, they will raise more or less contentious possibilities of arranging or rearranging things socially. Once such possibilities begin to be entertained and discussed we can say that politics has made its appearance.

Political issues are the matters which may come up for decision or review in the course of political activity. Perhaps the most basic one is the question of whether a society should have a formal state apparatus at all: this is the question raised by the anarchist. But there are a great variety of issues over and beyond this Archimedean query and it is with these that the present chapter will be concerned. I shall take in turn the civil, the economic and the legal sectors of society and investigate in each case the sorts of issues that arise there, assuming that there is to be a formal structure of authority. One point to note is that the issues discussed are all internal to the organisation of the society. I ignore the questions that arise about the way the society ought to behave towards other societies in the present and towards the societies that its own future generations will constitute: that is, questions about international and intergenerational arrangements.

There are three sorts of issues which come up with civil life:

14

how far the practices of this part of social behaviour should be reordered legally, how far they should be legally reinforced, and what means should be adopted to implement such reordering and reinforcement. The first question arises because some of the habits of civil life may come to seem unsatisfactory under scrutiny and legal interference may then appear to be desirable. For example, if it turns out that members of a minority group are treated as less than full persons in ordinary civil practice, government may feel obliged to propose legislation for curbing, so far as possible, the discriminatory treatment involved. Again, to take a very different sort of case, if there is a civil practice of families' adopting unwanted infants and the practice leaves it unclear whether the mother can reclaim the child, legislation may be introduced to settle the matter one way or the other.

Most of the questions which arise in the civil area have to do, not with how far to reorder existing practices, but with how far to reinforce them. As we know from the last chapter, every practice has a degree of moral support, nearly everyone being given some reason to want deviance discouraged by the expectation that others will usually conform. Unlike legal and economic practices, civil ones confer a status, that of being a person, which is held more or less equally by all of those who possess it. This means that the measure of support which they receive should be correspondingly more reliable. And so it is. The persons in a society may come to be significantly alienated from the economic or legal patterns that they sustain, but it is unlikely, except for special and limited circumstances, that they should ever withdraw the support of their moral approbation from practices such as non-violence, non-fraudulence, truth-telling, promise-keeping or benevolence. These practices establish a dispensation of respect and the ending of this, unlike the ending of an economic or legal regime, would mean a more or less serious loss, if not to every individual or group in the society, at least to every recognised person.

But although the civil practices of any society may be expected to have a powerful informal backing, it may well be thought that some of them ought to be legally copper-fastened. In order to ensure that non-violence is nearly universal, many will agree that it should be given legal as well as moral support, offenders being subject to the rigours of the law as well as the barbs of public opinion. The reinforcement issue in the civil area of politics has to do with how far this process of legal buttressing should go. How many civil practices should be left to the mercies of popular advocacy? And how many should be given the stamp of official backing?

Just to comment briefly on this issue, nearly everyone will agree that non-fraudulence, like non-violence, ought to be given the sanction of the law, but the questions become more difficult to adjudicate as we look at truth-telling, promise-keeping and benevolence. Here those issues arise that are often discussed under the title: law and morality. Should lying or welching be punishable in law? Well, on occasion: in a court of law or after a formal contract, for example. And is marriage one of the occasions when promise-keeping should be legally enforced? Is marital infidelity to be legally tolerated? Or marital dissolution? The mention of marriage pushes us on to some difficult cases that arise under the heading of benevolence, cases also engaged in the law and morality debate. It is often alleged that behaviour which challenges in any way the standard attitudes to marriage constitutes a breach of benevolence and ought to be prohibited in law. On this ground it has been proposed at one time or another that each of the following should be outlawed: extra-marital intercourse, homosexuality, prostitution, pornography and even artificial contraception. There are two inquiries to be made about such forms of behaviour. The first is whether they may genuinely be regarded as offences against benevolence, whether they can really be seen as harmful. And the second is whether they should be banned, even if they are judged to be such. Discourtesy is for certain an offence against benevolence but no one has suggested that it should be proscribed in the statute books of the law-makers.

The third issue which comes up in the civil area also arises elsewhere. Even when decisions have been made on the reordering and reinforcement that the law should provide for civil life, there remains the question: by what means ought it to impose this regimentation, with what sanctions ought it to penalise trespass. Here again we touch on a well-probed region of debate. What is the point, and what ought, therefore, to be the pattern, of punishment? Is the aim of legal penalties to make retribution for wrong-doing or is it something more tangible, such as one or a mix of the following: to reform the offender, to deter others from following his example, to protect society from further offences that he might commit, to make compensation to his victim? So much for the point of the exercise. And when we have determined it, there still remains the question of its pattern. Do we allow physical, even perhaps capital, punishment of offenders? Do we make use of prisons or only of institutes of rehabilitation? How much scope do we leave for the imposition of fines and do we ever direct these to the compensation of the victim? And, finally, are we to rely on part-time community service as a means whereby an offender can make up for his misconduct? This hornets' nest is as familiar as the law and morality one.

In the economic area of social life the same three types of issue come up as are occasioned by the civil. The most important one by far is the reordering question, but before dealing with it we can put aside the other two. Reinforcement is not an issue so far as the economy goes because it is universally accepted that without legal backing no economic practice can be expected to survive. The sanction of moral disapproval is not likely to ensure continued conformity to any given practice, for as we have seen the fruits of conformity are almost inevitably distributed to the greater advantage of some than others; even while everyone continues to have some reason for wanting deviance to be discouraged, the temptation to flout moral opinion and to take what belongs to another must become irresistible for the relatively dispossessed. Thus we find that a question is rarely raised about how far economic practices that have not already been subjected to legal reordering ought to be legally reinforced: it is assumed almost on all sides that every one of them ought to receive the buttressing of the law.

The issue of means is just as significant in the economic sector as it is in the civil, but there is not much more to say about it here. As in the other case the questions we have to consider are: what do we hope to achieve by levying sanctions on those who transgress the legally regimented economic practices; and, granted this aspiration, what sanctions do we think will help us to bring about our goals. One point to note in this case is that in a developed economy the powerful economic agents are bound to be institutional rather than individual persons and that the punishment of institutions can hardly take any of the traditional forms, other than that of the fine. Some economic offenders, as indeed some civil, will inevitably be institutional and it may be that political consideration should be given to novel means of penalising them; the fine is all too often a very light burden for a powerful economic organisation to bear.

The issue of how far the state ought to go in reordering existing economic practices takes us to a centre of contemporary political debate. Since the appearance of classical economic theory in the eighteenth century there have been advocates of *laissez faire*, proponents of the view that the state so far as possible ought to keep out of the economy. On the other side there have been believers, from Marx and earlier, in the supreme desirability, and even historical necessity, of the state's assuming total economic control. The ground between these extreme positions has also been staunchly maintained, the disciples of the mixed economy being no less enthusiastic than opponents in their theoretical attachments. It is not our task, happily, to adjudicate the debate between these parties, although we shall eventually be considering the criteria on which it ought to be resolved. Our only job at the moment is to put the controversy in perspective, throwing light on the general issue of how far the state ought to reorder the economy.

The first way in which reordering comes about is almost inevitable in any large-scale society. If the state, in the form of legislature, judiciary and executive, is to operate at all then it must have some means of meeting the costs involved: that is, of paying its officials and organising its enterprises. This has almost always meant that the state becomes a tax collector, and collecting taxes already involves some reordering of the economy. Thus there is no way in which governmental interference in economic affairs can be avoided.

The costs of essential state operations might prove to be relatively trivial, however, and so it is possible to hope that the taxation will not cut deeply into the existing distribution of property. However, there are two other purposes besides their own maintenance which states have widely sought to fulfil, on the basis of taxation, since the sixteenth century. The first is the provision of non-marketed goods, and the second the relief of the poor.

Non-marketed goods are those which are made available to the members of a society other than through the market mechanism; they are paid for by government out of tax revenue and distributed *gratis* to the public. Why should government go to the trouble of organising the provision of these commodities? In some cases the reason, and it has been found compelling nearly everywhere, is that the items are so-called public goods: they benefit everyone if they benefit anyone, and cannot therefore be marketed, yet the benefit is not so great that any individual or group can be expected to take on the burden of providing them. An example of such a public good, or at least of an alleged public good, is the protection of one's country against aggressors. Everyone supposedly benefits from the security that an army provides, yet that benefit is not so great that any individual or group will think of meeting the cost, even if it could do so, on its own. Other cases which resemble this one are: prevention of violence and other aggression on the public streets, inspection and control of potential sources of disease, information on the likely state of the weather some time in advance, and research into technological possibilities of ameliorating human existence that are not likely to be commercially investigated. With public goods of these kinds it is very natural that government should tax members of the society so as to pay for the goods out of the revenue collected. Theoretically it may be possible that members should get together voluntarily to provide the commodities, but since the contribution of any one among a group of voluntary subscribers is not likely to be crucial to the success of the venture there would always be a temptation for a pledged subscriber to fail to do his bit and to free-ride on the efforts of the others. Thus it has been widely accepted, even among *laissez faire* thinkers, that the state ought to foot the bill out of the funds yielded by compulsory taxation.

But the non-marketed goods that states have widely sought to provide are a broader class than that of public goods, strictly defined. Other commodities are provided out of tax revenues because marketing them is thought to be difficult or is held to have undesirable side-effects, although which goods are put in these categories varies from one society to another. In most societies government takes on responsibility for the printing of money, the provision of a transport network, and the development of public parks. In some the process goes much further and we find for example a national education system, a national health service and a national insurance scheme. In all of these cases government takes over a role that could, at least in theory, be filled by a private entrepreneur. The money could be printed by private banks, the roads and railways built by companies seeking a profit through fares and tolls, the parks provided by leisure enterprises which charge entry fees, and so on.

Apart from maintaining its essential operations and providing certain non-marketed commodities, the state in most societies has also pursued a third purpose requiring taxation. This is the relief of the poor: the redistribution of income, in however limited a fashion, from the wealthy to the needy. The needy in contemporary western societies are held to include the elderly, the incapacitated, the overburdened and the unemployed, but the category has elsewhere been more narrowly defined. The point that needs to be made, however, is that the function of redistribution has rarely been neglected entirely by modern states and that it has supplied a further justification for the reordering of the economy which taxation represents.

As a tax collector, then, we can see that, to a greater or lesser extent, the state interferes willy-nilly with the way existing economic practices work out. But our survey of its scope of operations in this regard enables us to see that almost inevitably there are two further respects in which it will also make its economic presence felt. One is, very simply, as a big spender. Having control over the conduct of a great number of transactions, whether in hiring personnel to fulfil its purposes or in making contracts with various supplementary agencies, it necessarily has a significant effect on how the economy works. And the second respect in which it gains a powerful presence is as the printer of money, if, as nearly everywhere, it takes that task into its hands. With the printing of money it naturally takes on responsibility for control of the money supply and, by a slight extension, control over interest and exchange rates. These powers are reins by which it can influence the direction and intensity of economic activity, and they give it a unique role in the economic sphere. The state is not just a tax collector and a big spender, it is also the society's bank.

Granted that so much reordering of the economy goes on inevitably in large-scale modern societies, it may well be wondered what the fuss is about in the *laissez faire* debate. Briefly, the question has to do with how far the state should involve itself, with the revenues that extra taxation can bring, in the provision of marketed goods. Should it subsidise companies within an industry by which the market has been doing badly, thereby saving jobs in a lean period? Should it perhaps buy out some companies in a given industry and compete, whether for profit-making reasons or in the interest of some higher good, with companies in private ownership? Or should it go one step further and buy out all competitors within the industry, or just close them down, thereby establishing itself in a monopoly position? These are the matters around which the contemporary debate turns. In most large societies of the present time we find some subsidy, some ownership and even some monopoly exercised by government in the area of marketed goods. The issue is whether this should be seen as a regrettable, if often understandable, economic interference, or as part of a praiseworthy development whereby enterprises on which the public welfare depends are taken into public ownership.

Let us turn now from the economic sector to the legal aspect of social life, the third area in which political issues are liable to arise. Here there is hardly a distinction to be drawn between reordering and reinforcing, since every legal practice is naturally up for consideration. There is just a single question of what pattern of legal practices should be enforced. Notice that because authority parallels ownership and is almost always distributed asymmetrically there is rarely a thought of leaving legal practices merely to rest on moral sanctions. Like economic practices the legal ones are almost universally given the buttressing of the law: a law, as it happens, that they make possible. The question of what pattern of legal practices to institute will receive all our attention here because, while there is the further issue of the sanctions appropriate for enforcing the practices in law, this raises just the same problems that we have already noted in the civil and economic cases.

The issue on which we have focused has been the major topic of much traditional political theory. We are asked to decide on the ideal form of legal practices, the form in which it is best that authority should be constituted. What ought to be the titles to legislative, judicial and executive authority? And what ought to be the corresponding rights? We describe a system as democratic, on the western use of the word, when the titles to the major legislative and executive roles come from free popular elections and when the rights of the executive are restricted so as to prevent interference with judicial decisions. In the United States all the legislators, the members of Congress, are popularly elected whereas in the United Kingdom only members of the house of Commons have to receive support at the polls. And in the United States the chief executive, the President, is popularly elected, while in the United Kingdom his counterpart, the Prime Minister, can claim such a mandate only indirectly, through being chosen by the popularly elected members of the lower House. However, although democracy allows of significant variations like these, perhaps the sharpest question in this area is whether or not the best legal system is a democratic one. Of course few thinkers will be found who defend non-democratic regimes under that description, but this is a reflection of the different uses to which the term 'democracy' is put; generically it always means 'the rule of the people', but in specific detail it may often have connotations quite removed from those which we have given it.

Since our task in this chapter has been merely to chart the variety of political issues we may rest with what we have achieved at this point. We have seen that the internal issues which come up in arranging legal practices *vis-à-vis* civil and economic ones can be nicely parcelled out in packages that correspond to the three sectors of social life. In the civil and economic areas we have the three issues of how far to reorder existing practices, how far to reinforce those not reordered, and by what means to impose these forms of regimentation. In the legal sphere the first two questions run together into the single issue of what pattern of practices ought to be established there but the question of means remains as important as it is elsewhere.

In conclusion, and in further summary, it may be useful to introduce the notion of a social charter or constitution. What a charter would do is to set out solutions to all the political issues that we have described in this chapter. It would describe a framework or pattern for the organisation of social life in its civil, economic and legal aspects, giving an account of what is due to persons, owners and authorities within the society, and of what sanctions may fall on anyone who fails to give that due. It would be impossible here to give an example of a charter in all the detail that it would necessarily involve but what we can do is to sketch

21

the broadly contrasted sorts of charter adumbrated in our survey of political issues. If we leave the penal issue aside then we can describe a contrasted pair of destinies for the organisation of each sphere of social life. Civil organisation may reinforce existing practices a little or a lot, depending on how the law and morality debate is judged; it may, roughly speaking, be liberal or illiberal. Economic organisation may or may not entail a significant amount of government involvement in the provision of marketed goods; it may, in equally rough terms, be socialist or non-socialist. And finally legal organisation may or may not give importance to popular election as a legislative and executive title and to the independence of the judiciary from executive control; it may or it may not be democratic. These different possibilities compound to give us eight varieties of social charter. If democratic, a charter may be socialist and liberal; or socialist and illiberal; or non-socialist and liberal; or non-socialist and illiberal. That gives us four types of charter. And if a charter fails to be democratic we get a corresponding four possibilities, giving us eight types of charter in all.

Bibliographical note

For a survey of the penal issue in politics a useful book is Ted Honderich, *Punishment: The Supposed Justifications*, Penguin, Harmondsworth, 1971. The rival sides on the law and morality debate are well represented by H.L.A. Hart, *Law, Liberty and Morality*, Oxford University Press, 1962, and Patrick Devlin, *The Enforcement of Morals*, Oxford University Press, 1965; Hart takes the liberal view. A useful source book is Louis Blom-Cooper and Gavin Drewry, eds, *Law and Morality: A Reader*, Duckworth, London, 1976. The socialism and democracy issues mentioned in the chapter are matters of such widespread debate that it is difficult to make recommendations. On the economic question it is still worth consulting Anthony Crosland, *The Future of Socialism*, Schocken, London, 1956, although the book is widely criticised on the left. Norman MacKenzie, *Socialism*, 2nd ed., Hutchinson, London, 1966, gives a short history of socialism. For a survey and discussion of the democracy question see Jack Lively, *Democracy*, Blackwell, Oxford. 1975.

3 The role of political philosophy

There are three problems which anyone who is anxious to make a political impact on his society will have to face; they concern, respectively, analysis, assessment and action. The problem of analysis is that of identifying the different arrangements in respect of political issues which are real alternatives to the *status quo*; here the important thing is to avoid the utopian mistake of neglecting constraints on social change and thinking that every imaginable charter is a feasible alternative. The problem of assessment is that of selecting from among the plausible options distinguished in analysis that charter which is superior to competitors; the task is to name one's preferred social ideal, to say how one thinks that one's society ought to be ordered. Finally, the problem of action, assuming that one's ideal does not coincide with the *status quo*, is that of deciding what and how much one ought to do in furtherance of the changes which one judges desirable in the organisation of social life. The first problem, analysis, belongs strictly to the scientific sphere; the second, assessment, to the philosophical; and the third, action, to the practical.

Our focus in this text is the properly philosophical member of this triad: the assessment of rival forms of social arrangement. The scientific task, roughly speaking, is that which dominates the efforts of political and social analysts, or at least such efforts of theirs as have a critical thrust, while the ethical project is the leading theme in the very practical debates carried on within groups of political activists. The job of assessment, to which we have to give our attention, is a more abstract enterprise than its partners and is not so easily located within the mansions of political thought; indeed it is a job that often goes by default, the scientists rushing the implications of their analysis, and the activists not examining the assumptions of their practice. What makes it distinctively philosophical is that it is concerned with that most traditional of philosophical aspirations: the goal of characterising the good society.

The remark invites elaboration. In selecting a charter of social life as superior to the alternatives in the field, one is naturally described as seeking out the best arrangement available. But in fact the job of political assessment is only rarely characterised as the search for the best or optimal form of organisation. What is more usually said is that the goal is a specification of the demands which justice makes on such organisation. It seems that the good society is not necessarily the best arrangement of social matters but an arrangement which, uniquely or not, succeeds in being just.

Despite the appearance there is no real difference between those who proclaim justice to be the matter of political assessment and those who represent that matter as the optimal society. The divergence of terminology comes about through an ambiguity in the idea of a social arrangement or form of organisation. That may refer to what we have called a charter for social life, a set of solutions to the different political issues, or it may suggest something much more detailed: a blueprint or model of a society in the totality of its features, not just political but also cultural, economic, technological, and so on. If we use the phrase in the first sense then it is perfectly reasonable to say that political assessment is bent on identifying the best arrangement of social matters, or at least the best family of arrangements. That description of the goal is commonly avoided, however, because it suggests, in a modulation to the second sense of the phrase, that the aim is to grade societies in an indefinite wealth of detail. At this point recourse is usually had to the concept of justice and the objective is redescribed as the characterisation of the just arrangement or family of arrangements. But we should not be deceived. The just charter, if there is a single outstanding candidate, is simply the best one, although being a charter, it may be compatible with many different forms of more concrete organisation. In what follows we shall speak indiscriminately of the best or just social arrangement as that which political assessment is concerned with identifying, for the term 'arrangement' and its associates will be used exclusively to refer to a charter.

There is more, it must be admitted, to the concept of justice in a social charter than that of the arrangement's being thought optimal, but not so much more as makes a significant difference. For justice and optimality to coincide, the criterion whereby best is judged must meet certain constraints. In particular, it must be one which looks in some broad sense to the interests of people and which does not place the interests of some above those of others in an arbitrary fashion: that is, in a manner for which there is no plausible justification. These constraints are quite naturally satisfied in judging which of a number of charters is best, since the point of view from which such judgment calls to be made is unlikely to be other than one of a concern with the interests of individuals; we are not often going to be concerned with which is best from an aesthetic or biological or even religious point of reference.

Putting aside the problems of analysis and action then, our focus in this discussion will be political assessment: the evaluation of competing charters of social life or, more modestly, of the rival solutions to one of the issues which a total charter would cover. We shall be concerned with how it is possible to find one's way rationally towards a particular assessment and preference, as distinct from stumbling on the position one adopts through a contingency of upbringing or association or loyalty. What we shall be seeking is a convincing criterion by appeal to which the case can be made for one charter or solution rather than others. The criterion should work as a base of adjudication between alternatives, a touchstone for determining which of a set of competing options is to be preferred.

The criterion which we are seeking for political assessment often goes under other names. One characterisation, favoured by John Rawls, would present it as a conception of justice. As we have seen, the concept of justice picks out as optimal a charter which serves people's interests in some allegedly non-arbitrary way. Building on this, Rawls says that a conception of justice gives flesh to the abstract concept and defines the matters which that concept leaves open: it identifies in specific terms the interests that a charter should serve and the manner in which it should serve them. On this account a conception of justice fulfils exactly the same role as the criterion that we have been describing. It gives one the desired base from which to argue that a charter is preferable to alternatives.

Other characterisations of our criterion for political assessment derive from welfare economics. One would present it as a social choice function whereby, given a set of competing charters or solutions, it would indicate a best member, or a subset of equally good best members. That is merely to redefine what is meant by criterion in slightly more technical language. Other descriptions from economics are more specific in their presuppositions. A somewhat outdated one, that of the social welfare function (in the Bergson-Samuelson sense), would suppose that the charter meriting preference guarantees something called social welfare that is mathematically computable in a certain way from data on the performance of the charter. Another, the social decision function, would assume that the best charter has the feature of answering in a particular way to the preferences of individuals over the alternatives available: say, that of being the choice of a majority among them.

The principal topic of contemporary political philosophy, and that which gives us our perspective in this textbook, has to do with the criterion that ought to be used in political assessment, providing an agreed base for argument. In seeking out such a criterion political philosophy does something that is also attempted elsewhere, for example in welfare economics and in jurisprudence. This, however, is no embarrassment, for there is independent evidence that disciplinary boundaries have been badly drawn in the area. And, if we have to justify the demarcations, we can always point out that political philosophy tackles the criterion problem at a more general level than the other pursuits: they are concerned respectively with excellence in economic performance and legal pattern, while no such restriction is put on the criterion that we are committed to find.

But we need an understanding in some greater detail of the form which a criterion for political assessment, a conception of social justice, might take. The most compelling shape, in some ways, is that which we find embodied in a slogan like the following: seek first freedom, then equality, and last of all fraternity. Here we have a set of distinct values mentioned in the criterion but the values are assigned strict weights *vis-à-vis* one another. The weighting comes by a serial ordering which directs that equality be introduced only to rank charters that have already passed the test of freedom, and that fraternity be applied only to the ranking of charters that have been found satisfactory on the score of equality. The variety of values recognised in such a criterion of justice makes for an intuitive appeal and the strict weighing of the values ensures that the criterion will not offend on the ground of offering ambiguous indications.

Very closely related to the serially constructed criterion is one which again mentions a number of different values but weights them in a scalar rather than a serial fashion. We would find such, for example, in a slogan that said freedom, equality and fraternity are all that matter, and they matter equally; or freedom, equality and fraternity are all that matter but freedom is twice as important as the other two. Slogans like this invite an arithmetical interpretation according to which the rival charters should be scored on the different value dimensions, in the prescribed ratios, and that charter selected which achieves the highest score. (On the picture envisaged there is a mathematically describable function which assigns their relative importance to the different values and picking the optimal charter means finding that arrangement which, because of the way it satisfies the values, yields the highest output for the function in question. Here it is appropriate to speak in the language espoused by some economists of maximising the output of the function in one's choice of charter.)

Serial and scalar criteria have in common the fact that they mention a plurality of values. When one comes across such pluralism in political philosophy then more often than not one finds that the weights attaching to the values are not specified. Thus the cry of the French Revolution was the simple: freedom, equality, fraternity; its authors omitted to indicate the pattern, serial or scalar, in which those values were to count. A philosophy which offers such an incomplete criterion of justice is often called an intuitionistic one, since the idea usually is that the weighting of the values in the assessment of rival charters, or in the adjudication of more concrete political options, should be left to the intuition of the person making the judgment. There are serious arguments in the literature of ethics and politics as to why intuitionism is the only plausible disposition on evaluation but this is not the place to examine them. What must be clear is that an intuitionist philosophy is a fall-back position, an outlook to which one should have recourse only in despair of finding a compelling, fully elaborated criterion of justice. The time to explore the approach, if it ever comes, will be when attempts to give political argument a firmer base have all proved unsuccessful.

Since they are closely related to intuitionism, it may be worth while in passing to mention two other political philosophies which proclaim despair on finding well-structured criteria of justice. One is the position described by Brian Barry as conservatism, the other an approach to which I would like to give the name consensualism. The conservative claim, associated classically with Edmund Burke and more recently with Michael Oakeshott, is that human reason is an imperfect instrument and that the search for criteria designed to guide political assessment is a futile and dangerous enterprise. It is futile because, removed from the natural support of an encompassing tradition, the mind cannot hope to be able to make sure judgments on the range of charters theoretically available in politics. It is dangerous because, not realising its futility, people may be encouraged by it in disruptive attempts at social criticism and reform: attempts the bad results of which may not allow of being put right.

The consensualist position is adumbrated in the work of the contemporary German social theorist, Jürgen Habermas. The guiding idea is that we can be no more confident of finding a criterion for directing political assessment than we have proved successful in describing a method for scientific theory choice; but that neither should we be less sanguine about the prospects of introducing rationality to this enterprise than we are about realising it in the other. In the scientific case one line of thinking has been that though we may not be able to spell out a canon of scientific argument we may reasonably endorse as rational those conclusions which scientists will be led to espouse in the long term of free inquiry and debate. The suggestion in the political case is that a parallel holds and that we may reasonably look with confidence to the decisions that people would reach on matters of justice were they allowed to negotiate the questions in a context free of distortion. We may not be able to isolate the ground or method which guarantees the rationality of any assessment reached with its help, but what we can do is to give a condition under which assessment may be expected to be rational. We can say that the just charter for a society is the arrangement that would attract consensus in an extended process of debate, assuming the debate to be free of the pressures of distortion: in a phrase, that the just charter is the arrangement that would command rational consensus. To say this, however, is not to point to a way of determining the just charter, for we can no more expect to anticipate the resolutions of our political debaters than we can hope to foresee the discoveries of scientists.

Conservatism and consensualism both resemble intuitionism in being pessimistic counsels and the question of whether they are compelling only arises when it has been established that no convincing criterion of justice is in the offing. Our task in this text is to look at the enterprise of searching out a criterion and so little more will be said on any of these doctrines. If a pessimistic conclusion is forthcoming from what we say then it will come by the general brunt of our commentary on attempts to formulate a criterion of justice, and not by any specific consideration of the pessimistic alternatives.

We have seen that a criterion used in political assessment may be serial or scalar, depending on how the values mentioned in it are weighted *vis-à-vis* one another. But, even more straightforwardly, a criterion may involve just one value by which to judge the alternatives up for assessment: it may be singular rather than plural. The enthusiast for liberty who cares nought for the equality and fraternity mentioned in the revolutionary cry does not have to worry about a weighting system, serial or scalar. If he is attached exclusively to this value then it gives him all that he needs in the evaluation of charters and other more contained political proposals. His libertarianism may not seem a very fetching political disposition but it is at least a determinate one; it avoids the ambiguity of indications attending an intuitionist formula. The same goes for the egalitarianism, or indeed the fraternalism, which someone might extract from the more articulated, if less efficient, French slogan.

Not surprisingly the pure, non-pessimistic positions in political philosophy are associated with singular rather than plural criteria of justice. Indeed the three philosophies discussed in this book offer just such uncomplicated yardsticks for political assessment. The first, the approach associated nowadays with Robert Nozick, presents legitimacy as the hallmark of justice: 'legitimacy', a term which I have introduced to the discussion, here connotes propriety in the way in which the system emerged, or at least in a way in which it could have emerged. The second philosophy, the utilitarianism deriving from Bentham and Mill, makes welfare into the touchstone of what is politically right: this requires that what is preferred in politics is always what produces the most happiness. And the third approach, that which is naturally linked with John Rawls, puts forward fairness as the criterion by which to distinguish the just charter or policy from the unjust: for Rawls this means that it is the charter or policy which anyone would have been happy to see introduced, had he not known what position he was going to occupy in the society to which it is introduced.

Political philosophies, at least when they eschew pessimism, are distinguished by the criteria of justice they put forward, be those criteria serial, scalar or singular. But it must be recalled in conclusion that the philosophical job is not so much to invent different criteria of assessment as to argue for one criterion or family of criteria above others. A philosophy has to be able to put a case for guiding political assessment by its preferred formula: it has to show that there is reason in ranking alternatives by legitimacy, welfare, fairness, or whatever, and that this is not one method of assessment among many. In the chapter that follows we shall be looking at the means whereby such a case can be made.

In the meantime let us recap briefly on what we have been through in this chapter. We saw that the focus of political philosophy was the assessment of rival social charters or rival solutions to one of the issues covered by a social charter: this, rather than political analysis or action. Such assessment, we noted, could be described in terms of pursuing the optimum or seeking justice, the distinction being irrelevant so long as it is clear that the evaluation is of charters and not of any more concretely specified forms of organisation, and that it is made from the point of view of the interests of individuals. The job of political philosophy is to provide rational guidance for this ranking of alternatives, describing a criterion by which the ranking can be performed. Putting aside pessimistic approaches such as intuitionism, conservatism and consensualism, we identified three sorts of criteria that might be put forward. The serial and scalar types involve a plurality of values but weight them differently; the singular criterion mentions just one value. The philosophies which we shall be considering in this book all present singular criteria, defining justice respectively as legitimacy, welfare and fairness.

Bibliographical note

On the concept of the good society see Anthony Arblaster and Steven Lukes, eds, *The Good Society*, Methuen, London, 1971; on the concept, and different conceptions, of justice John Rawls, *A Theory of Justice*, Oxford University Press, 1972; and on welfare economists' ways of characterising criteria Amartya K. Sen, *Collective Choice and Social Welfare*, Oliver & Boyd, London, 1970. Intuitionism is well described in Rawls's book, pp. 34–40. The best recent presentation of an intuitionist outlook is Brian Barry, *Political Argument*, Routledge & Kegan Paul, London, 1965: here the use of indifference curves is recommended as a means whereby the intuitionist can make his judgments scrutable. Barry gives a short account of conservatism in *Political Argument*. The recent classic source of the doctrine is Michael Oakeshott, *Rationalism in Politics*, Methuen, London, 1962. For an account of the consensualist position associated with Jürgen Habermas see Philip Pettit, 'Habermas on Truth and Justice' in G. H. R. Parkinson *Marx and Marxisms*, Harvester, Brighton, forthcoming.

4 The method of political philosophy

The role of political philosophy is to give rational guidance in the evaluation of rival institutional arrangements, to describe an argumentative case for political assessment. This it will do if it can offer a criterion for deciding between any alternatives that may be presented, whether at the level of overall charters or at the level of rival solutions to a particular issue. But how can the political philosopher make a case for his preferred criterion against the many competitors in the field? How can he show that his measure of justice is the right or true or appropriate one? This is the question with which we shall be concerned in the present chapter.

The first thing to notice about political philosophy is that, as we have described the enterprise, it is a reflective, rather than an empirical, form of inquiry. What is meant by this is that the data which it has to investigate in the pursuit of its goal are not materials of observation such as would have to be sought out in the laboratory or the field. In order for the political philosopher to gain access to those matters with which his theory, his account of the criterion of justice, will have to accord, he has to go in for reflection, not research. He has to think about the criteria available for political assessment, the virtues which they may be held respectively to realise, their ramifications for judgments of justice on various institutional possibilities, and the fit or lack of fit between those ramifications and his untheoretical responses to the arrangements in question. It is such reflection, if anything, that may be expected to reveal to him the propriety of invoking one or another criterion in the evaluation of political options.

The data of political philosophy are usually distinguished into two categories. On the one hand the philosopher is said to be able to rely on certain judgments or intuitions about matters of principle, such as that all human beings are equally deserving of personal respect, or that people are entitled to keep for themselves what they produce without the aid of others, or that the only thing worthwhile in itself is the happiness of rational beings. On the other he is held to be in a position also to rely on certain considered judgments about more or less particular matters, such as that slavery is wrong, arbitrary arrest unjust, and religious repression indefensible. Both sorts of data are made available through reflection and it appears that in constructing his theory, his version of the criterion of justice, the philosopher has to satisfy, so far as possible, the conflicting demands that they make.

If we are to understand the method whereby a political philosopher can argue to a preferred criterion then we need a model of the interaction between a theory of the sort that he seeks and reflective data such as these. What I propose to do is to present a model of the interaction between a regular scientific theory and the empirical data to which it is supposed to relate; and then to consider how far something analogous to that model applies in the reflective case on hand. The exercise will prove to be beneficial for it will lead us to an illuminating picture of reflective method, and a picture, moreover, which picks up many of the points commonly made about how political philosophy should go about its business.

Before we look at our model of empirical theory-construction an important remark has to be made. This is that political philosophy is only one among a wide range of reflective disciplines. Other studies of the kind include logic, linguistics, aesthetics, decision theory and, perhaps the closest relative, ethics. What is distinctive about this group of inquiries is that while they have to square with often recalcitrant data, those data are supplied by reflection rather than research. The disciplines are marked off from mathematical inquiries by the fact that they are not purely deductive exercises and they are distinguished from empirical investigation through not relying mainly on findings in the laboratory or field. Where political philosophy relates to judgments bearing on institutional justice, logic concerns itself with judgments on validity in arguments, linguistics with judgments on sense in sentences, aesthetics with judgments on beauty in works of art, decision theory with judgments on rationality in choices and ethics with judgments on goodness in actions. In their development it is true that some of these disciplines have become more or less mathematical but at least in their initial motivation they share with political philosophy the characteristic of trying to make theoretical sense of data revealed to the inquirer in personal reflection. Thus, if they are to perform their respective tasks, the logician must be able to tell a sound argument from an unsound one and the linguist must be able to distinguish a grammatical from an ungrammatical sentence: otherwise they have nothing to reflect on and attempt to explain.

The model of empirical theory-selection which I shall present derives from an analogy elaborated by Mary Hesse between a theory and a learning machine. The idea is that we should think of a theory as if it were a computer-like machine which learns in interaction with its environment, an environment that provides a continual flow of data. What the theory has to do is to record and classify the data, subsume the observations made under a manageable set of general laws and use these laws to project future events, indicating what is likely to happen under different circumstances. The theory will be successful, establishing a stable equilibrium with its environment, if it develops such laws that it can handle any new piece of data coming in and make novel projections that succeed in being fulfilled.

The analogy with the learning machine suggests that we credit the theory with at least three distinct components: a receptor, a theoriser and a projector. The receptor takes in the data provided by the external environment and processes them, delivering to the theoriser a set of sentences which represent, in terms of a given stock of predicates, the events observed. The theoriser takes in these sentences and seeks to display them as instances of general truths so that something like 'A *P* was found to be a *Q*' gets marked off as yet another example of the law that 'All *P*'s are *Q*'s'. Finally, the projector takes these generalisations from the theoriser and applies them to a predictive purpose, spelling out what may be expected to happen in various concrete circumstances. These predictions, corroborated or undermined, become part of the empirical input which is delivered to the receptor: when they are borne out, the theory's representation of the environment is vindicated; when they are falsified, the picture must be looked at again and amended.

What interests us mainly about this model of an empirical theory is the types of amendment which it allows us to envisage in face of recalcitrant data. Suppose that it is recorded at some point that a *P* is not a *Q*, contrary to the theory's laws and predictions, and consider now the different sorts of response that may be made within the theory in order to accommodate this striking piece of evidence. The following are four moves, in increasing order of significance, to which resort may be made. (1) The observation may be held to have been a case of mistaken identity: what was not a *Q* was not a *P* either, or what was a *P* only seemed not to be *Q*. If later attention or experiment can be tolerably well

33

squared with this response then this move may succeed; otherwise it must be displaced in favour of a more radical response.

(2) The stock of predicates on which the receptor draws may be revised somewhat so that a *P* of the sort that was found not to be a *Q*, for example, is held no longer truly to be a *P* and the generalisation 'All *P*'s are *Q*'s' is saved. This move, it should be mentioned, is facilitated by a feature of empirical theory which we did not make explicit above, that the predicates employed in the receptor will usually have been tailor-made to the sort of theory produced by the theoriser. There is no natural, stable language of observation but only languages which already reflect certain theoretical dispositions and so it may be quite easy to revise some terms in such a language in the cause of saving a theory. Move number 2, however, will not always be successful. If it is to work then there must be some general feature of the troublesome *P* whose presence in entities that would otherwise have been taken to be *P*'s is found on at least some occasions to go hand in hand with their failure to be *Q*'s.

If the second sort of move fails then resort will be made to the third or fourth, both of which take us from the receptor to the theoriser. (3) The law which the troublesome piece of data affects, or some related law, may be amended so as to allow for the observation. For example 'All *P*'s are *Q*'s' may be revised to read 'All *P*'s under condition *C* are *Q*'s', where *C* is a circumstance that was not realised on the occasion of the anomalous observation. Or, to mention another possibility, it may be that the *P* in question was held not to be a *Q* on the grounds that it was an *R* and there is a law to the effect that 'No *Q*'s are *R*'s': in this case move 3 may consist in the rejection or modification of this other law. It is a feature of theory that the resort to our third ploy may take the form of amending any one of a number of laws; the law most directly challenged by a bothersome observation may not be that which is chosen for revision. But the third move, however carried out, may not always prove to be successful. It is more than an abstract possibility that no variety of adjustment will restore a stable equilibrium between the theory and its environment. What may happen is that, short of stooping to highly artificial *ad hoc* alterations, it will not be possible to isolate the theory from rebutting pieces of evidence.

In this case we may expect to find the last and most radical response to a theoretically troublesome observation. (4) What is held up now for questioning is one or another aspect of the framework of suppositions within which the original theory was conceived. The distinction between the suppositions and laws of a theory – often represented as that between the theory's ontological and empirical content – is a distinction of degree: suppositions are marked off by the role they play as constraints on the form of laws entertained in the course of research. Nevertheless it is important, as can be appreciated from considering some such candidates for the status of suppositions as, in physics, the principle that the causes of all material events are material, the principle that the material world does not vary structurally as we move about in space or time or the principle of the conservation of energy. The fourth response to recalcitrant evidence is to scotch some supposition or set of suppositions involved in one's theory and to start again, so to speak, from the beginning. Einstein made such a fresh start, for example, when he gave up the Newtonian assumption that there was an absolute spatial framework relative to which states of rest and motion could be defined.

So much then for the method of theory-selection in the empirical sciences. What we must now ask is whether there are any respects in which theory-choice in the reflective sciences exhibits a similar methodological structure. The answer is that such respects abound. The most cursory consideration of the learning machine picture suggests a parallel model for the selection of theories in political philosophy and in other reflective inquiries. It allows us to see how the political philosopher may expect to corroborate a given account of the criterion of justice and to undermine the alternatives offered in its place. And it gives us a similar insight into the methods of vindication available to the logician, the linguist, the aesthetician, the decision theorist and the ethical thinker.

To begin to spell out the suggested picture, we can see a reflective theory as bearing to a range of personal judgments a relationship of the sort that empirical theory bears to an area of observed facts in the natural or social order. Those judgments are supplied for each discipline by the theorist's reflection on what he, assuming that he is competent on the matters in question, would naturally say: that is, on what it would be natural for him to say after a modicum of consideration, not on what he would spontaneously blurt out. The logician's judgments deal with validity, the linguist's with sense, the aesthetician's with beauty, the decision theorist's with rationality, the ethician's with goodness and the political philosopher's with justice. These judgments are the raw material of the respective inquiries and they make up a fair bulk, for the stock can be increased indefinitely in each case, the inquirer seeking out his considered judgments on more and more cases, however hypothetical and imaginative.

Faced with the appropriate judgments, a reflective theory will seek first to classify them, then to reduce them to a smaller number of general laws or principles and finally to use those principles to project further judgments which ought, in consistency, to prove themselves avowable: they ought to be judgments which match the theorist's intuitive responses. Thus the theory, in fair parallel to its empirical counterpart, will have a receptor, a theoriser and a projector and it will allow, in response to considered judgments that do not fit its projections, any of the four sorts of amendment described in the other case. A recalcitrant judgment, it can be supposed, may suggest criticism of the original observation, the theorist considering whether he can really have got his own intuitive response correctly. And equally plausibly, it may occasion revision of the terms in which it was classified; amendment of one or another of the principles that it threatens; or, in the last resort, abandonment of some of the suppositions within which the unstable theory was conceived. Thus one can conceive of a logician having before him an indefinitely extendable range of judgments on the validity of certain sorts of argument, and exploring all the avenues we have just described in the struggle to identify a manageable set of principles embodied in the judgments.

But we must consider in particular how the picture applies to the enterprise of political philosophy. Here the goal is something less articulated than a set of logical principles for predicting which arguments will be found on consideration to be valid, or a set of linguistic axioms for forecasting which sentences will be judged, after reflection, to be sensible. The aim is a criterion, as short perhaps as a single principle, by which the theorist will be able to tell whether or not an institutional arrangement is just, the criterion pre-empting the particular judgment which consideration confirms that he would support. Although the theory sought out in political philosophy is of such a relatively straightforward kind, the structural parallel with disciplines like logic and linguistics still goes through. In this case, as in the others, the data base is given by the unrestricted range of judgments to which the theorist is intuitively disposed, and the job of the theory is to provide intellectual control over that stock of judgments, extricating a principle or principles that they embody.

The picture suggested is highly compelling. The political philosopher begins with certain judgments of which he feels quite certain such as, to give our earlier examples, that slavery is wrong, arbitrary arrest objectionable, and religious repression unjust. He wonders whether he can find a common principle or set of principles underlying these: an interesting criterion which gives a reason why each phenomenon should be seen as unacceptable. Suppose that he comes up with a hypothesis: a tentative criterion, such as that individuals should only be restrained when they perpetrate harm on others. His job then will be, first, to see whether this principle fits the original judgments and, second, to see whether its further ramifications accord with judgments that he is intuitively disposed to make. If the hypothesis fails either test, and cannot readily be accommodated, he will search out another, until eventually he hits upon a criterion in equilibrium with his considered intuitive responses. With this in hand, he can then predict what he will find just and unjust and can reinforce his intuitions where before they may have sometimes been less than certain. The pattern is very persuasive, being the parallel of what we see elsewhere in the reflective disciplines.

And yet there is a difficulty. At the beginning of this chapter we mentioned that the judgments to which political philosophy has been held traditionally to be responsive are of two kinds: judgments about matters of principle and judgments about more or less particular affairs. The model which we have been elaborating supposes, it would seem, that the important judgments for a political philosophy to come to terms with are those of the second, more specific kind. We are invited to think of the theorist seeking out a principle or set of principles which sums up the pattern in his judgments on the justice or injustice of this or that or the other institutional arrangement; we are discouraged from seeing him as responsive to intuitions on matters of a general kind. The parallel with other reflective disciplines reinforces this effect, for in those cases it does seem to be only the particular judgments that operate in constraining the theories.

What are we to say about this? Well, first of all, in order to mitigate the difficulty raised it is worth pointing out that the learning machine model leaves room for the influence of general suppositions as well as specific observations: and this, even in non-reflective science. Recall that a theory was said to be developed under the guidance of background suppositions that determined the sorts of law which ought to be expected. In parallel to this we may imagine our political philosopher seeking to satisfy his general intuitions in the form that he gives to his budding criterion of justice, as he tries to match his intuitions on particular matters in the content that he allows the criterion to assume. It is important to any philosopher that such general intuitions reinforce the criterion he offers, for otherwise he must conclude that there is no interesting reason why the principle accords with his particular judgments, and that it is mere accident that the formula serves as a way of summing up those judgments. In fact all the political philosophers considered in this text take their criteria to generate appropriate consequences because of expressing a feature which, intuitively, is deeply connected to justice. Because the criteria satisfy certain general intuitions of appropriateness, their protagonists present them, not merely as convenient ways of *generalising* particular judgments of justice, but as essential methods of *grounding* them.

So much by way of softening the difficulty raised. On the other side it is as well to admit that the method characterised may put less weight on intuitive judgments of a general kind than it does on judgments about more particular matters. The admission is easily made because judgments on matters of principle are abundant in a degree that encourages suspicion. Indeed, they are as often jointly incompatible as they are individually plausible. Isolate the case sufficiently and it is remarkable how intuitive any general idea relating to justice can be made to seem. That happiness is all that matters, that people are entitled to keep what they produce, that human beings are all equally worthy of respect: taken on its own each of these propositions seems eminently compelling. And yet in most worlds it turns out that the propositions will offer contradictory political recommendations. It may be as well that the method we embrace does not put a particularly heavy weight on such perplexing counsels.

These remarks will make it clear that the method prescribed for political philosophy rejects the *a priori* approach that would seek a foundation for the theory of justice in first, indubitable principles. There are no such principles in the area, or anywhere else for that matter: even the high level suppositions guiding theory choice may come on our model to be revised. But those who reject a rationalistic foundationalism elsewhere sometimes go for an empiricist foundationalism in its place, arguing that theory has an indubitable starting point, albeit a starting point for induction rather than deduction, in the deliverances of observation. It may be worth mentioning that such an alternative view is countenanced neither in our model of empirical theory-selection, nor in our picture of how reflective theories are corroborated. The learning machine analogy suggests that just as the guiding suppositions of a theory can be called into question and dropped, so observations can be redescribed and revised. Finding a stable theory means satisfying a flexible set of constraints, part observational, part suppositional, and none of these constraints can be regarded as irresistible. If the best way to get an overall theoretical fit is to recast some cherished principle or some compelling report, then so much the worse for the principle or the report. Nothing is immune to reconsideration; nothing serves as unquestioned foundation.

Political philosophy appears then to fit the reflective version of the learning machine model, even to the extent of rejecting a foundation in intuitions about matters of principle or indeed in judgments of a more particular kind: in general it may try to match the latter judgments but an important leeway is available, as it is available in empirical theory, on the questions of whether to countenance, and how to categorise, such data. One point remains to be made about the accuracy of the model, and it bears further on the revisability of those particular judgments which give political philosophy, or any reflective discipline, its data. In empirical inquiry, revision of an observation means a reconsideration of its reliability: if it was a one-off event, the assumption is made that the circumstances were misleading, if it is recurrent, confidence is withdrawn from the sort of perception, or the mode of apparatus, in question. The corresponding revision in a reflective discipline is rather more readily forthcoming.

The reflective theorist can alter a judgment with which an otherwise smooth theory jars, and he can do so without having to put doubt on sensory or external conditions. He simply decides, in the interest of finding a system in certain of his intuitive judgments, that he does not after all wish to say that such-and-such or so-and-so; previous intuitions on the matter are put down to lack of clear insight. On such a ground logicians have urged that 'All X's are Y's' does not entail that there are any X's, and linguists that 'Ideas sleep furiously' is ungrammatical. And, even more obviously, political philosophers have argued in the cause of maintaining their theories that consequences which otherwise they would have found counter-intuitive should in fact be tolerated. It is all too often that philosophers, presented with consequences of their views that seem to make for a *reductio ad absurdum*, outsmart their opponents by promptly embracing those results. Without condoning such an extreme practice, it is reasonable to allow political philosophy to employ a modicum of data revision, at least with the less compelling and possibly confused intuitions, in the attempt to find a unifying criterion of justice.

This completes our characterisation of reflective method, and in particular of the method of political philosophy. But it leaves unmentioned an important matter on which it will be useful to make a concluding comment. The term 'judgment' may be understood in either of two senses, sometimes distinguished as the 'act' and 'content' interpretations of the word. On the act interpretation, a judgment is a mental event, an act of judging; on the content, it is a received fact: what it is that is taken to be so in the act of judging. This ambiguity runs systematically through our discussion of the reflective disciplines, for it was left unclear whether a reflective theory is an attempt to find a system in the judging performances of the theorist, considered as events of a mainly subjective significance, or as a project of discovering a pattern in the matters judged by the theorist to be so: this, on a stricter parallel with empirical science, which looks for a pattern in the things observed to be so in the laboratory or field. The first reading makes the theory a systematisation of the subject's practice, the second a story about how things are in the public realm to which his judgments give him access.

How one reads reflective theory affects considerably the status which one attaches to it and the interest which one finds in it. The one construal gives it a purely instrumentalist status, making of it a tool for pre-empting particular acts of judgment. If the theory says that justice is legitimacy, for example, that is not supposed to be something true or false, it is a formula whereby we are enabled to know in advance how the theorist, and those who think like him, are liable to judge on political issues. The other reading gives reflective theory a realist or cognitive status, representing it as a distillation out of intuitions about a certain objective realm which has the merit of revealing a structure hidden in the welter of more or less particular, and in great part unrelated, judgments. On this account, a theory which says that justice is legitimacy is held to pick up a pattern in those objective facts about justice of which our intuitive judgments give us an unsystematic record.

If one reads a reflective theory on instrumentalist lines, and the point applies as much to the other disciplines as it does to political philosophy, then the interest it will have for the theorist is as a decision procedure: a means of by-passing deliberation on the particular matter under consideration and coming to an immediate decision. On the other hand, if one reads it on realist lines, its interest will be cognitive: the theory will be held to offer an insight into how things in a certain area are. Notice that given the first account, the theory will be of direct interest only to the theorist himself and to those who are like him, and it will be of indirect concern to anyone wishing to know about these people. Given the second, the theory aspires to be of universal significance, or at least of significance to anyone who broadly agrees in the particular judgments of the theorist which supply the theory's data base. How far the theorist may expect to secure such agreement, and in particular whether agreement may be expected across cultural barriers, is a controversial question and we shall say nothing on it here.

But what is to determine whether a reflective theory should be read in an instrumentalist or a realist fashion? The answer to this query would take us into deep matters of epistemology and semantics. Those who espouse an emotivist or prescriptivist analysis of evaluative statements will tend to go for an instrumentalist reading of political philosophy, since they cannot give cognitive significance to judgments of justice; those who defend a cognitivist account of evaluative utterances will probably, if they countenance the enterprise, interpret it in the realist fashion. Since the matters engaged in such analyses outrun the concerns of this book, I propose to leave unresolved the question of whether to read political philosophy, or any other reflective theory, in a realist or instrumentalist manner. All that follows in the text will sustain the ambiguity which we noted in the term 'judgment' and will be compatible with according a theory of justice either of the available construals.

To recap then on the ground covered in this chapter, we began with the remark that the data of political philosophy are given by reflection rather than research, a feature which puts it in the company of other reflective disciplines like logic, linguistics, aesthetics, decision theory and ethics. We took from Mary Hesse an account of empirical theory-construction based on the analogy of a learning machine and then we extended this to the process whereby reflective theory is corroborated. The outcome was a picture of political philosophy as seeking to develop a criterion which matches in its consequences at least most of the judgments of justice that we find intuitive; it will also seek to satisfy intuitions on matters of general principle, but that is a less significant constraint. This picture identifies as the most convincing criterion of justice the formula which, in a phrase introduced by John Rawls, is in reflective equilibrium with our considered judgments on particular issues of justice. Finally, we took notice of the fact that our account of the method of political philosophy, and indeed of any reflective discipline, leaves open the question of whether to interpret its results in a realist or instrumentalist manner.

Bibliographical note

The learning machine model of theory-construction in the empirical sciences is given in Mary Hesse, 'Models of Theory Change' which appears in Patrick Suppes *et al. Logic, Methodology and Philosophy of Science*, Amsterdam, 1973. Related matters are discussed in her book *The Structure of Scientific Inference*, Macmillan, London, 1974. The picture of method in political philosophy is close to John Rawls's account of reflective equilibrium developed in *A Theory of Justice*, Oxford University Press, 1972, although Rawls, at least in explicit methodological comment, downgrades the role of general intuitions. It also squares with the comments on method in that great utilitarian text, Henry Sidgwick's *The Methods of Ethics* (1874), Macmillan, London, 1962, and with the methodological remarks in Robert Nozick, *Anarchy, State and Utopia*, Blackwell, Oxford, 1974. Rawls himself claims that Sidgwick endorses the method of reflective equilibrium but this is contested in Peter Singer, 'Sidgwick and Reflective Equilibrium', *The Monist*, vol. 58, 1974. Singer rightly points to a greater reliance in Sidgwick on intuitions about matters of general principle than reflective equilibrium would encourage. But Singer's comments are distorted by his assumption that the appropriate reading for political philosophy as understood on the reflective equilibrium model is the instrumentalist one. Someone who makes a distinction connected with that between realism and instrumentalism, and relates it to the reflective method, is Ronald Dworkin in *Taking Rights Seriously*, Duckworth, London, 1978, chapter 6. He does not think that realism allows the revision of intuitive judgments, which we have countenanced, perhaps, because he fails to recognise that some of our intuitions may be quite plausibly taken as the issue of unclarity and may, on that account, be made candidates for revision. For an account of the realism-instrumentalism issue about values, one which is untypically sympathetic to realism, see David Wiggins, 'Truth, Invention and the Meaning of Life', *Proceedings of the British Academy*, vol. 62, 1976. In a recent paper Norman Daniels recommends a wider understanding of reflective equilibrium, an account which resembles ours in not putting exclusive reliance on the fit between theory and intuitions about particular matters of justice. He also shows awareness of the realism – instrumentalism issue. See 'Wide Reflective Equilibrium and Theory Acceptance in Ethics', *Journal of Philosophy*, vol. 76, 1979. Among methodological remarks from elsewhere in the reflective sciences it is worth mentioning the comments on the method of inductive logic in Nelson Goodman, *Fact, Fiction and Forecast*, 3rd ed, Bobbs Merrill, New York, 1973, chapter 3. David Miller in *Social Justice*, Oxford University Press, 1976, rejects outright anything like the method of reflective equilibrium. He argues that there are three incompatible ways of interpreting justice, by reference to rights, or deserts, or needs; that the judgment between these is a judgment between different views of society; and that this latter judgment cannot be justified in a convincing manner.

Part II Individualism in political philosophy

5 Individualism and institutionalism

Although they are the major options available on the contemporary intellectual scene, all of the political philosophies considered in this text are individualistic. They hold in common that the purpose of social institutions, where institutions may mean groups or practices, is to serve the interests of individuals and they agree further that such institutions are intrinsically perfectible: they offer no resistance of themselves to being adapted to individual interests, although there may be other constraints on the adaptation possible. This reformist viewpoint represents groups and practices, in a metaphorical but not unwarranted characterisation, as playthings in the hands of people: instruments whereby individuals can better achieve their personal satisfactions. Not all institutions are supposed to have been the conscious product of individual ingenuity, but all are subject in principle to the ingenuity of the political planner.

Such an individualistic attitude will not go unquestioned. On the other side of the sociological fence are many who will reject the pretensions of our political philosophies as liberal naïveté. The point will be made, whether in a reactionary or revolutionary spirit, that social institutions are not merely conveniences fortuitously made available to the individuals who live beneath their sway; that they are the very means whereby those individuals are socialised and given a consciousness of themselves. To frame the questions in the terms of our own analysis, it will be asked how individuals who rely on institutions for their understanding of what it is to be a person, to have property, or even to exercise power, can be thought to be in a position to judge those same institutions from on high. The brunt of the questioning may be to either of two effects: that groups and practices, the heritage of history, are every bit as important as passing individuals and make a call on the allegiance and loyalty of political planners; or that they are so powerful in the control that they exercise over individuals that it is folly to think of interfering with them piecemeal, in the manner adopted by such planners. In either case it is likely that the natural world will be rifled for the imagery of living things with which it can feed the characterisation of institutions. We shall almost certainly be treated to an excursion in social physiology, as groups are made to assume the appearance of organisms, and practices that of deeply ingrained instincts. In this *tour de force* individuals will quickly shrink to the proportions of the cell and before very long we shall be contemplating in society a burgeoning form of life quite remarkably contrasted with the tranquil realms that we earlier described.

So characterised, the criticism of individualism may seem absurdly rhetorical. The rhetoric serves a purpose, however, dramatising an issue on which it is easy to drift uncritically into the orthodox, individualistic attitude. Nor is it entirely unjustified for, although it is a varied tradition, resistance to individualism has had frequent resort to biological metaphors. One strand in the tradition is the romantic cult of community or nation and this, whether in Hegelian tone or not, speaks of the spirit pervading and directing the society as though it were the soul imagined by vitalists to be the principle of life in the organism. Another strand is the historicist one which sees the development of societies, be the pattern linear or cyclical, as the outcome of iron laws, these laws being modelled on the regularities dictating growth, decay and regeneration in living things. A third strand, perhaps nowadays the most important one, derives from sociology and usually takes a functionalist form according to which each society ensures in the changes that occur within it that the overall function of its preservation is fulfilled. Again the underlying metaphor here is biological, for the paradigm of the self-regulating system is the organism in which evolution has guaranteed appropriate responses to threatening conditions: perspiration when the temperature gets dangerously high, adrenalin when a hostile attack is imminent, and so on.

The individualism attacked in this tradition is a shared supposition in the political philosophies that we shall examine. It plays a role in those philosophies of a kind that physicalism fulfils in science, putting serious constraints on the form envisaged for the criterion of justice. We saw earlier that any political philosophy will be constrained by intuitive assumptions on certain matters of principle, assumptions such as that happiness is all that counts in the end or that human beings are equally worthy of respect. The individualistic supposition plays a much deeper constraining part than any assumptions of this kind could reasonably aspire to take on, for while the political philosopher may pick and choose among the latter, he scarcely has an option about espousing the constraint of individualism.

This remark may seem strange after our characterisation of a non-individualistic tradition: a tradition often referred to as collectivism or holism, but which we shall describe as institutionalism. Might a political philosophy not explore the possibility of replacing individualism by this alternative constraint? I think not, since institutionalism would undermine the concern with the interests of individuals by which political philosophy has been distinguished: this concern we mentioned in chapter 3. In theory an institutionalist might consider the evaluation of alternative institutional arrangements; his point of view will tend to be not the interests of individuals, but the smoothness of the society's operations, the consistency of the operations with traditional patterns, or whatever. Such evaluation is made to seem gratuitous, however, when we remember that institutionalism casts doubt on the perfectibility of institutions as well as on their purpose *vis-à-vis* individuals: it suggests that they may not be responsive to the efforts of planners to change them. In practice the doctrine has meant the death of the political disposition or it has encouraged one of two distinctive outlooks: the reactionary one of resisting social planning, related to the conservatism mentioned in the chapter before last, or the revolutionary one of applauding planning only when it harnesses existing patterns of change.

To simplify drastically, institutionalism has been the social theory of reactionary Burkians and historicist Marxists. Whatever Edmund Burke himself thought, it has been the claim of many who identify with him that society is a natural historical growth with a primacy over the individuals who are its members and that only mischief is brought about when those individuals seek to meddle in something that is not of their making. On the other side many Marxists, though scarcely Marx himself, have argued that since people are the product of their age and can only form political ideas which reflect exigencies of their environment, the attempt to work out those ideas for purposes of critique and reform is a uselessly parochial one. The problems of any age up to the emergence of the classless society are only properly solved when the economic basis of the society shifts and a new period is ushered in. All that people can do that is of real political significance is to collaborate with history, so far as the laws of history are revealed in Marxist science.

In contrast to the inertia or extremism that institutionalism fosters, individualism supports the disposition enshrined in the search for a criterion of justice. It licenses the concern with the interests of individuals and it reinforces confidence that institutional arrangements can be made to serve those interests better than they do. This individualist outlook comes originally from the smithy of the bourgeois revolutions: the resistance in England, America and France to the claims of the feudal order. And as it was forged there, so was the contemporary tradition of political philosophy. Individualism and the enterprise of formulating a criterion of justice are indissoluble, the one from the other. The political philosopher, to return to the thought suggested a little while ago, has no option but to espouse an individualistic constraint on his theorising.

Once we grant this conclusion we are faced with the question of whether individualism can be vindicated. Unless the doctrine can be shown to be a reasonable view to adopt, we can scarcely consider it worthwhile to investigate the pathways charted by political philosophy. The task of considering the merits of individualism must be postponed, however, until the next chapter. What we shall do in the remainder of this chapter is to try to identify and define the central issue that divides the individualist from his opponent.

We have already said that individualism asserts, first, that the purpose of institutions is to serve the interests of individuals and, secondly, that institutions are intrinsically perfectible so far as fulfilling that purpose goes. Either of these tenets, we suggested, may be questioned by the institutionalist critic. So described, the doctrines seem to be embroiled over a rag-bag of not very clearly defined issues. No conditions have been laid down on what are to count as the interests of individuals, for example, and no exact sense has been given to the notion of the perfectibility of institutions. There is clarificatory work to be done. One approach to the clarification might be to provide exact definitions of the matters that have been left vague. But that would still leave a rag-bag of questions dividing the rival doctrines, albeit a rag-bag of well-defined questions. Instead I propose to take another route to clarity, which is to probe beneath the issues that we have mentioned, in the search for something more basic, and perhaps more straightforward, that puts the competing theories at loggerheads.

Specifically, I want to suggest that the real matter of contention between individualism and institutionalism is an ontological one: it concerns the entities that should be countenanced as part of the social scene, and their status *vis-à-vis* one another. The adherents of both doctrines admit that individuals and institutions – that is, groups and practices – are both portions of the furniture of society, but the individualist denies that institutions are anything over and beyond individuals: he thinks that groups are nothing more than the people who belong to them and that practices are nothing more than the actions in which they are respected. The institutionalist argues against any such reductionism, suggesting that groups and practices are autonomous entities whose presence is something distinct from the presence of individuals, and something just as powerful.

As characterised in this way, the issue offers a nice sociological parallel to the problem which plagues discussion in philosophical psychology: that of whether mental states and events are anything over and beyond material ones. The main options in the psychological case are monism and dualism. The one view would say that what we identify as a mental operation is just a material occurrence in the brain, if it is anything at all: one and the same operation may be identified in mentalistic terms or in the terms available to the neurophysiologist. The other view would deny such identity and hold that while mental states and events may always be attended by neurophysiological counterparts they are nevertheless distinct entities. Monism corresponds neatly to individualism, and dualism to institutionalism. In the sociological area, as in the psychological, the issue is whether two distinct departments of thought represent one and the same realm of reality under different aspects, or whether they correspond to equally distinct regions of being.

That the ontological issue is the core of the dispute between individualism and institutionalism will need some argument. I do not say that it is the explicit topic of debate between those doctrines, so far as they touch on political matters. Nor do I say that a position on the issue is logically entailed, in the strict sense, by the things that either party to the dispute has to say. My claim is that rival commitments on the ontological question are the motivating reasons behind the claims which the individualist and the institutionalist respectively make. It is because he thinks of institutions as involving nothing more than people that the individualist unquestioningly takes them to be answerable to the interests of individuals, and regards them as artifacts which can be made and unmade according to design. And on the other side the reason, plausibly, why the institutionalist finds one or both of these assumptions objectionable is that he imagines groups and practices to have a mode of being beyond that which they borrow from individuals. He thinks it an unwarranted piece of naïveté, granted this independence, to depict institutions as instruments of human satisfaction which are subject to the will of individual agents.

I mean to take it, then, that the central argument between our rival doctrines concerns the issue of whether institutions are onto-logically autonomous relative to individuals. But this still leaves us short of the clarity that we desire. The sense of ontological autonomy in question is scarcely luminous and the attempts that we have made to spell it out are distressingly metaphorical. To say that autonomy means that institutions exist over and beyond individuals, or that they have a mode of being other than that which they borrow from individuals, may be suggestive but it does not give us much real insight into the issue under discussion. In what follows I hope to put this lingering obscurity right and to extricate a sharply defined question for analysis in the next chapter.

There are two plausible accounts of what ontological autonomy means and they provide rival criteria by which it may be judged. These accounts, these criteria, I will denote respectively as the expressive and the explanatory. The expressive criterion says that one sort of entity X exists over and beyond another sort Y if, and only if, the following condition is fulfilled: that the addition of terms by means of which we refer to X-type things enables us to give expression to truths that we cannot formulate in a language with terms for referring to Y-type items. The idea is that if we have two sets of referring terms, the one for things of sort X and the other for things of kind Y, we can tell whether the X terms refer us to things other than Y-things, or to Y-things under a novel aspect, by seeing whether the referring use of X-terms increases our expressive resources. We may ask for example whether sentences exist over and beyond the words which make them up. The criterion says that they do, so long as referring to them as well as to words – that is, using the concept 'sentence' referringly as well as the concept 'word' – enables us to express more things than we could before. (Notice here that while the criterion might deny ontological autonomy to sentences *vis-à-vis* words, it would not follow that autonomy would also have to be refused the other way around: there might yet be things expressible if we refer to words as well as to sentences which cannot be expressed by reference to sentences alone. This is as we should want, for where one sort of entity, sentences, seems to presuppose another, words, we may want to say that the sentences are nothing over and beyond the words without implying that neither are the words anything over and beyond sentences.)

What do we say of institutions relative to individuals on this expressive criterion of autonomy? Does referring to institutions as well as to individuals enable us to express truths that we could not have formulated before? The answer, unfortunately, is not something on which there is common agreement. Some philosophers have defended a translational variety of individualism according to which anything that can be said by referring to groups and practices can equally well be said, if only at greater length, by referring to the people who make up those groups and conform to those practices. Against this others have urged that no amount of paraphrase into the terminology approved by the translational individualist would allow us to give expression to what we report when we say that the mood of the country is changing, or that the trades unions are regaining confidence, or even that someone cashed a cheque at his bank.

The problem with judging the proper answer to the translational question is that no very clear standard is available for measuring when the same truth is expressed in different terminologies. Notoriously this difficulty comes up in translation from one natural language into another and it is no less sharp here, where we are considering translation from a rich language with concepts for referring both to individuals and institutions into an austere one deprived of the means of securing reference to the institutional entities. I am willing to allow that we should be as demanding in our judgment of attempts at such reductionistic rendering as we would be in assessing translation from French into English. And, allowing this, I am willing to admit then I cannot see how we can fail to find fault with the efforts of translational reductionists. There is no individualist rendering I can imagine which would satisfy me that it had caught the sense of saying that someone cashed a cheque at his bank, a remark in which there is an explicit reference to an organisation and an implicit one to the practice underlying the writing of cheques.

If we go along with this line of concession then it seems that on the expressive criterion for judging such matters we must say that institutions are entities that exist in their own right, over and beyond individuals. Fortunately, the conclusion is not a difficult one to accommodate. The sort of autonomy granted to institutions must also be accorded to sets *vis-à-vis* their members and to abstract properties relative to their possessors, and such a thin-blooded autonomy is scarcely sufficient to underwrite the institutionalist's disposition, that is, his attitude towards the individualistic claims about the purpose and perfectibility of groups and practices. If we consider three objects on my desk and now, enriching our terms, refer to the set which they constitute, we find that there are things which we can then say that could scarcely have been expressed before: such as, for example, that the set has three members, or that it satisfies certain mathematical axioms, and so on. Again, if we think about the approximately rectangular table and now refer to the rectangularity in its own right, it turns out that we thereby increase our expressive resources, opening up such propositions as that the approximate rectangularity is something with unusual geometrical characteristics, that it is not a shape that has launched a thousand ships, and so on. An autonomy that is found as much in sets and shapes as it is in social life is not the sort of quality to encourage the institutionalist or to worry the individualist. We may conclude that neither is it the sense of autonomy that lies in the background of our debate.

The second account of ontological autonomy is the explanatory one. This formally mirrors the first, saying that one sort of entity X exists over and beyond another sort Y if and only if the following condition is fulfilled: that the addition of terms by means of which we refer to X-type things enables us to give explanations of events that we cannot explain in a language with terms for referring to Y-type items. In this formulation I assume that to explain an event is always to reveal something about its causal ancestry. The idea then behind the criterion is that the X-terms refer us to things other than Y-things, and not to Y-things under a novel aspect, if with their help we are pointed towards causal connections that had escaped us before. To put the matter more crudely but more intuitively, the entities to which the X-terms refer exist over and beyond the Y-type entities if, and only if, they have irreducible causal powers. With sets and members both allowed within our objects of reference we may have greater expressive resources at our command than with sets eliminated, but it does not seem that we have greater explanatory ones, at least not in the stipulated sense. Reference to sets does not enable us to account for any happenings that are unaccountable if we are only allowed to refer to the members of the sets. In no plausible sense do sets have distinctive causal powers: that is, powers which are not simply the properties of their members.

Here is the criterion of ontological autonomy which lies at the back of the debate between individualism and institutionalism. What has to be determined is whether reference to groups and practices allows us to explain events which are inexplicable by reference to individuals alone. The question is whether such institutions have causal powers of their own, whether they are forces whose agency does not reduce to the doings and responses of individual people. More rhetorically still, it is the old matter of whether men alone are the makers of history, or whether we must also allow for the efficacy of impersonal agents. In the chapter that follows we shall consider how the argument about the issue is to go and we shall see if the individualism presupposed in the enterprise of political philosophy can be vindicated.

In this chapter we have seen that all the political philosophies to be considered later are individualistic in assuming that the purpose of institutions is to serve the interests of individuals and that institutions are intrinsically perfectible so far as fulfilling that purpose goes. The opposite of such individualism is institutionalism, an outlook which either kills the political disposition or encourages a reactionary or revolutionary attitude. The issue between the two approaches boils down, we argued, to a difference on the ontological question of whether institutions are anything over and beyond individuals. We then saw that this dispute can be understood in either of two ways, depending on whether ontological autonomy is measured by an expressive or an explanatory criterion. The explanatory criterion seems to be the one in question and so we now have to consider whether institutions have causal powers that are irreducible *vis-à-vis* the powers of individuals.

Bibliographical note

The forms of institutionalism described at the beginning of the chapter are so rhetorically characterised that it is hardly fair to ascribe them to particular authors. A sense of what they claim can be gleaned from Steven Lukes, *Individualism*, Blackwell, Oxford, 1973. James Coleman notes the emasculation of political philosophy that contemporary functionalism would sponsor in 'Social Structure and a Theory of Action' in Peter Blau, ed., *Social Structure*, Open Books, London, 1976. The individualistic assumption that institutions are meant to serve the interests of individuals is closely tied to what Brian Barry sees as the liberal picture of social co-operation, according to which people cooperate because it benefits them to do so: this, rather than because of hierarchical pressures or altruistic motives. See the epilogue to *The Liberal Theory of Justice*, Oxford University Press, 1973. For a short but illuminating account of ontological questions see the last chapter of Mary Hesse, *The Structure of Scientific Inference*, Macmillan, London, 1974. The *locus classicus* of a relative of the expressive criterion, according to which 'to be is to be the value of a bound variable', is W. V. O. Quine, 'On What There is', reprinted in *From a Logical Point of View*, Harvard University Press, 1953. The causal account of event explanation which is supposed in the explanatory criterion is discussed in my paper 'On Actions and Explanations' in Charles Antaki, ed., *The Psychology of Ordinary Explanation*, Academic Press, London, forthcoming. Finally, the general issue between individualism and institutionalism is more fully discussed in Graham Macdonald and Philip Pettit,

Semantics and Social Science, Routledge & Kegan Paul, London, forthcoming, chapter 3; in particular the case for allowing the expressive autonomy of institutions is made out there in some detail.

6 The case for individualism

The question before us now is whether we can present an effective argument against the ontological claim by which institutionalism is distinguished. Can we make a case against the view that by referring to institutions we are enabled to explain happenings which are inexplicable by reference to individuals, institutions having irreducible causal powers? Unless we can do so then it will seem gratuitous, at the least, to describe the purpose of institutions as one of serving the interests of individuals, and to assume that institutions are intrinsically perfectible in respect of that purpose. And in that case it will hardly appear to be worthwhile to explore attempts to formulate a criterion of justice that have supposed precisely such reformist tenets about institutional purpose and perfectibility.

I believe that we can argue effectively against ontological institutionalism, but the argument will only persuade those who acknowledge the approximate truth of what I shall call the humanistic or orthodox conception of human agents. The argument is to the effect that such a view of people does not allow one to countenance the claim that institutions have distinctive causal powers. The conception of agents in question banishes the thought that reference to institutions might enable one causally to explain things which cannot be explained just by reference to individuals; it is straightforwardly incompatible with an institutionalist doctrine of that kind. But what is the orthodox conception of human agents? I take it to be the picture of people with which we work in our daily life, as we wonder at what we ourselves and others do, and find our way to this or that story about the matter. The orthodox conception is the common framework of ideas which enables us to distinguish an action from a mere reflex; to put forward a plausible account of the genesis of an action in one or another state of the agent's mind, and to project the other responses that may be expected of an agent who adopts that way of looking at things.

The ideas in the framework are the familiar ones of perception and judgment, assumption and theory, inclination, wish and ideal, policy and intention, reason and motive, and so on through a readily extendable list. To be master of these concepts and an expert in the application of the framework one needs to have taken on, tacitly if not in an explicitly theoretical commitment, certain assumptions about the nature of action and its relationship to antecedents. In what follows I shall attempt to spell out some of these, although not in great detail. We must have a good sense of what they are if we are to understand the humanistic or orthodox conception that gives us a base for arguing against institutionalism.

The major humanistic assumption is that any event which counts as an action comes about as the result of a state of mind which, in a phrase of Donald Davidson's 'rationalises' the behaviour. If we use 'belief' and 'desire' as catch-all terms, then we can say that an agent's state of mind rationalised a given action *a*, if he desired in bringing about *a* that he should perform an action with a certain property *p*, and if he believed that *a* would certainly or probably have that property. That an event is rationalised in this way, that it displays such behavioural rationality, is what it means for it to count as an action. Thus behavioural rationality is not something that someone who qualifies as a human agent is liable to lack; nor indeed is it something that is likely to come in degrees, one person having more of it than another. This is rationality in a sense in which it is a constitutive property of human beings, or at least of human beings who have not entirely lost their senses; it may not be sufficient for humanity, being ascribable to some other animals perhaps, and indeed to angels, but it is certainly necessary for it. We assume behavioural rationality as a matter of course in the performance of anything that we regard as an action. The event is an action only if there is a certain sort of explanation to be given of it, and the explanation that we seek is always, at least at one level, an account in terms of what the agent was after and what he thought he was doing, that is, an account which refers us to a belief and desire state that would have made it rational for him to do what he did.

A second humanistic assumption about people is that beliefs and desires, to continue to use catch-all phrases, are at least in the general run intentional and, being such, that we cannot say what someone believes or desires just from seeing the things with which he is presented. A mental state is intentional in the relevant sense when two conditions are fulfilled. The first is that the state is properly identified, not by some intrinsic mark such as its feel or effect, but by reference to that which counts, in a common phrase, as its object. Beliefs and desires meet this condition because which belief or desire is at issue in a discussion is always settled by the appropriate object: the state is the belief or the desire *that such-and-such* or *that so-and-so*. The other condition on an intentional state is that if the object is differently charac-terised then reference to it will pick out a different state. This rather vaguer constraint is met by at least most beliefs and desires, for plausibly we preserve the same object if we swap a co-extensive or synonymous term for a word in a that-clause, but making the swap will normally mean that the clause picks out a different belief or desire. The belief that the lawn is coming on cannot strictly be the same as the belief that the sward is coming on since it may be true that someone believes the first and false that he believes the second.

An important consequence of the intentionality of beliefs and desires is that we cannot tell what someone is thinking or wanting just from the things presented to him: even if we knew that his faculties were directed to a particular object, say a table, we would be in ignorance as to how that object was taken by him, whether as something solid, a piece of mahogany, a priceless antique, or whatever. This means that the agent's circumstances leave us free to ascribe any of an indefinite range of mental states to him, and in particular that we can attribute such states as make rational sense of the actions that he performs. The assumption of behavioural rationality and the assumption of intentionality are well matched in this respect.

A third humanistic supposition about people, and it is the last that I shall mention, suggests some partial but important con-straints on what someone is likely to believe or desire; these, in combination with the evidence of his actions, determine the men-tal states that we ascribe to him. It is supposed that the agent's beliefs and desires are at least partially responsive to pressures of practical and theoretical rationality. To be practically rational is to take account of all one's interests and inclinations, both in one's own regard and in regard to others, when allowing a desire to issue in action; it is not to be so selfish or short-sighted, for example, that one frustrates more of one's desires than one sat-isfies in performing a particular deed. To be theoretically rational is to pay attention to counter-examples, inconsistencies and other infelicities in forming and extending one's beliefs; it is not to be so obtuse that these pressures, being ignored or disregarded, fail to affect the pattern of one's commitments. Our third supposition is that human agents are subject to the norms of theoretical and practical rationality and that if they are entirely insensitive to them then they must be out of their senses or not human after all. The assumption is a light constraint, however, since we are fully prepared to admit that all sorts of non-rational pressures may also have an effect on the things which people come to believe and desire. We readily allow for the warping influence of inertia, self-interest and indoctrination, passion, social position and personality.

So much by way of describing the humanistic conception of agents. What can we say now in the way of justifying it, for justification is desirable if the conception is to give us our base against institutionalism? The most important thing to say is that in our everyday accounting for what we and others do we are all of us humanists, even if we differ culturally in other significant respects. This may not seem to be much of a warrant, however, since folk theories of things, even theories as entrenched as the humanistic conception of agents, do not have a good track record in the history of science. Perhaps our favoured conception may prove with the development of psychology to be just a passing prejudice in the history of the species.

This possibility takes us into a very deep issue in the philosophy of the human sciences and I can only deal with it briefly here. There are two things which I want to say. The first is that so far as can be seen the humanistic view of agents is as irreplaceable as our habit of interacting with one another after our present fashion. Interaction with a person is distinguished from intervention in a natural causal system by a host of features, one of the most central of which is reciprocity. This quality means that I depend on my overtures' having their desired effect on you, through your understanding what effect it is that I desire to achieve. If such reciprocity is to be preserved as a characteristic of human interaction then it seems essential that we maintain our humanistic conception of one another. It is only because we conceive of one another as forming and holding beliefs and desires in the way which that view characterises, that we can assume the appropriate reciprocity in entering mutual interactions.

But what if neurophysiology comes up with an alternative, and much more systematic, scheme for explaining and predicting behaviour? Would that not show our conception to be wrong? I do not think so. Being able neurophysiologically to scrutinise the brain and behaviour of another would not enable me to interact with him: no more than taking the engineer's view of a computer, examining the state of core at each stage, would enable me to play chess with it. If I am to interact I must put aside my neurophysiological equipment and return to the humanistic point of view, just as I must ignore the electronic data and treat the computer like any other opponent if I am to play chess with it. Thus to maintain the practice of interaction, and it is truly obscure how we could fail to do this, would necessarily be to assume that the neurophysiological theory did not after all undermine the humanistic conception: that the two representations of human beings were compatible.

The second thing which I want to say in justification of the humanistic conception is that not only is the conception irreplaceable, it is also unrevisable, in so far as it resists the sort of development enjoyed by scientific theories. This point is important because someone might hold out the prospect of psychology's regimenting the conception, much as decision theory does already, and then putting it through cumulative revisions in response to scientifically structured experiment and investigation. What is distinctive about the humanistic view, very briefly, is that it does not offer any means whereby we might establish ever more precise, and perhaps revolutionary, connections between people's beliefs and desires on the one hand and their actions on the other. The assumption of behavioural rationality forces us always to take an action to issue from a rationalising mental state and this fact stands as an impassable barrier to the procedure which we might expect of a scientific psychology. It undermines the possibility of the psychologist's finding action-independent indices of mental states and then investigating correlations between states so identified and actions. Any scheme proposed will topple as soon as a supposedly lawlike correlation runs into conflict with the assumption of behavioural rationality, predicting an irrational action. The most reasonable methodological response in such a case will always be to scrap the scheme and take the action, if it comes about, as rational, recasting the picture of what the agent's beliefs and desires were. To do otherwise would be to reject the main plank in a perfectly workable model of agents. More important, it would be to do this gratuitously, since the model allows that any action-independent indices of intentional states are unreliable, and since there is nothing obvious to be gained by sticking to the proposed indices and ceasing to assume that agents are behaviourally rational.

These concise remarks must suffice as a defence of the humanistic conception of agents. With that view of human beings characterised and justified, we must now look to the promised argument against the ontological claim of institutionalists. The argument is to the effect that one cannot consistently hold by the humanistic conception and come to believe that reference to institutions enables one to explain certain events that are inexplicable by reference to individuals alone. If one accepts the assumptions about agents which we set out above one cannot entertain the thought that institutions have irreducible causal powers.

The first premise in our argument is that any event which institutions might be invoked to explain is of a kind that the orthodox conception of agents would have to explain by reference to the mental attitudes of human beings. The idea is that for any event which the institutionalist holds to be inexplicable except by reference to groups or practices, the humanistic or orthodox conception will suggest a perfectly individualistic explanation by reference to the beliefs and desires of appropriate agents. There are two main varieties of events to be considered. One is the event which consists in the occurrence or the outcome of a certain sort of behaviour on people's part. Here the event must be held to be explicable in terms of agent attitudes, so long as the behaviour is taken to be action in the proper sense and not merely the triggering of autonomic responses. The other relevant variety is the event which consists in the occurrence or the outcome of a certain institutional change. If we take it again that the behaviour involved is a case of action, this sort of event must be held to be individualistically explicable on the following assumption: that anything describable as an institutional change is also describable as a change at the level of individual behaviour. The assumption is justified by our account of groups as composed of people, and practices of actions: a change in either must mean a change in its constituents, as surely as an alteration in a body of water must entail an alteration in its molecules. Thus it appears that our first premise is vindicated, and that any candidate for explanation by reference to institutions is also a candidate for explanation in terms of the beliefs and desires of agents. The only possible route to the rejection of the premise is the claim that the behaviour involved in the event is merely the triggering of autonomic responses in people, but that is not a fetching path to follow. If the institutionalist says that institutional explanations are relevant only to that behaviour in which people's attitudes are not rationally involved, then by the common application of the orthodox conception he shrinks the relevance of the scheme to vanishing point. Institutionalism is nothing if it is not a challenge to the orthodox manner of explaining a significant range of social events.

The second premise in our argument is even less controversial than the first. It is that if the institutionalist says that there are some events which can be explained by reference to institutions, but not just by reference to individuals, then he is denying the truth of the orthodox conception of agents. At least with respect to the behaviour involved in those events he is saying that it is not the rational outcome of the agent's beliefs and desires: and this, despite not restricting that behaviour to what might pass as autonomic responses. That he must be saying this is clear from the fact that if the behaviour were the rational outcome of such attitudes, then it would be explicable by reference to individuals, something which the institutionalist denies. Thus, where our first premise showed us that institutional explanations bear on events which the orthodox conception aspires to cover, the second makes the point that to hold such explanations indispensable in some cases is, therefore, to deny the claim of the orthodox conception.

The third and final premise in our argument is that the claim of this conception is undeniable, a premise which comes directly from our reflections on the irreplaceability and unrevisability of the conception. It follows at once that the thesis of institutionalism must be false, and that there are no events such that having the means of referring to institutions enables us to explain them when otherwise we would be at a loss as to their causal origin. It may be that reference to institutions gives us expressive resources which outstrip those available to us from reference to individuals, but so long as we attach ourselves to the orthodox view of agents we cannot think that it provides us with indispensable resources of explanation.

In order to illustrate the force of this conclusion, the brunt of our individualism, consider a standard sociological explanation, such as the explanation of the breakdown of the feudal manorial system by the introduction of money into peasant transactions. Here the event explained is an institutional change, the breakdown of a certain sort of group, and the explanation refers, among other things, to the practice associated with the introduction of money. By our first premise we know that the event explained involves behaviour such as the orthodox conception of agents aspires to encompass. And so it does: the breakdown of the manorial system is a change in the actions of those traditionally involved in the system, in particular a change in the pattern of peasant behaviour. This event is explained by reference to the introduction of money and the institutionalist might say that it cannot be explained just by reference to individuals, thus denying the ability of orthodox accountants to explain it in terms of the attitudes of the peasants: this denial is what the second premise draws attention to. But, as our third premise assures us, it is manifestly possible to make sense of the behaviour in orthodox terms, and so the claim of institutionalism must collapse. The introduction of money enabled peasants to attain certain hitherto impossible goals and created conditions within which they came to have desires and make demands that caused the demise of the manorial system. Such a story, and I am simply repeating the received version, trades in precisely the attitudes to which the collectivist would deny explanatory power. We are referred to the individuals involved, their beliefs and their desires, in having the behaviour explained that meant the fall of the manor.

So much then for the presentation and illustration of our argument against institutionalism. In conclusion, I would just like to mention that the institutionalist may argue at this point on the following lines: that while we may be able to explain events such as those under discussion by reference to the attitudes of individuals, this explanation requires reference to institutions in its full elaboration. In particular, the institutionalist will claim that we must refer to institutions in accounting for the attitudes, and even indeed in characterising them. He will point out that in characterising many of the attitudes of the peasants we used terms for institutions, speaking for example of their belief that monetary payment promised certain prospects, and he will say that if we are to account for the peasants' having such attitudes we must make further reference to institutions, putting down the formation of the attitudes to a causal interaction between the peasants and the institutions with which they were confronted.

We cannot give full consideration here to the objection raised but we can at least indicate how it may be rebutted. First of all, it must be said against the institutionalist that in characterising the attitudes of the peasants we do not strictly refer to institutions, although we may use terms for institutions in the characterisation. What we refer to are the attitudes themselves and it is more or less incidental that the content of the attitudes – what the individuals believe and desire – cannot be adequately specified without the use of terms for the institutions. We have already seen that a language with institutional terms will be expressively richer than one without and so, if the attitudes of agents in a society are formed in such an enriched vocabulary, it can be no surprise that we have to help ourselves to the vocabulary in order to characterise the attitudes. But using the terms for institutions in explanation of behaviour does not mean referring to what the terms would denote in non-oblique usage. If I say that an X brought about a such-and-such I am certainly referring to the entity in question, but if I say that someone's belief that an X is a so-and-so brought about a such-and-such I am only referring to the belief, and not at all to the X. This is brought out by the fact that I may not myself even believe that there are such things as X's: the claim may have been that someone's belief that a ghost was in the attic caused amusement in the company.

But if we do not refer to institutions in characterising attitudes that have an institutional content, our opponent may yet claim that we have to make reference to institutions in explaining the formation of such attitudes. If an object is perceptually salient, in the sense that consistently with the perceptual cues and circumstances it is inevitable that the percipient identify it in some sense, then we may reasonably say that a causal interaction between that object and the percipient accounts for the attitudes held in respect of it to which the perception gives rise. If I see the water in the pan bubbling and come to believe that it is boiling, then it is not unreasonable to say that my belief is occasioned by a causal interaction, specifically the interaction characterising perception, between the water and me. The idea proposed by the institutionalist is that a similar interaction between people and institutions must be postulated to explain the formation of certain attitudes which the people hold in respect of the institutions and that we have to refer therefore to the institutions in accounting for that formation. However, the idea is surely unpersuasive. Institutions are not perceptually salient objects, for it is not inevitable that they will be identified under certain cues and circumstances: it will always depend on the percipients' having appropriate collateral beliefs, such as the belief that such-and-such treatment is typical of group behaviour, or that such-and-such reasoning is indicative of conformity to a practice. The perceptual interaction, therefore, that lies at the base of certain attitudes which agents form in respect of institutions is not interaction with the institutions themselves but with those items which they take as evidential tokens of the institutions. Thus we are no more required to refer to institutions in explaining the origin of the attitudes which agents hold about them than we are in characterising the content of those attitudes.

This has been a tougher philosophical chapter than anything so far, and it may even be the toughest we shall meet. We began with a discussion of the humanistic or orthodox conception of agents, identifying it by assumptions bearing on the behavioural rationality of actions, the intentionality of beliefs and desires, and the practical-cum-theoretical rationality of agents. We argued that this conception, embodied in our everyday practice of making sense of ourselves and one another, is relatively indispensable, through its connection with interaction, and that it is distinctive in so far as it resists revision through scientific regimentation. With the humanistic conception thus enshrined in our cognitive affections, we went on to argue that the ontological claim of institutionalists is incompatible with it. To make that claim is to regard an event as explicable other than by reference to the normally operative beliefs and desires of people, when the event is of a kind that the humanistic view would naturally trace to just such attitudes. If we are to be humanists then, as I think we should be, we cannot but espouse the ontological doctrine of individualism: we cannot but maintain that whatever causal powers belong to institutions accrue to them by virtue of the properties of individuals.

Bibliographical note

The humanistic conception of agents is discussed in my papers 'Rational Man Theory' in Christopher Hookway and Philip Pettit, eds, *Action and Interpretation*, Cambridge University Press, 1978, and 'Rationalisation and the Art of Explaining Action' in Neil Bolton, ed., *Philosophical Problems in Psychology*, Methuen, London, 1979, but it is fully defended only in Graham Macdonald and Philip Pettit, *Semantics and Social Science*, Routledge & Kegan Paul, London, forthcoming. The argument against individualism is presented at greater length in Macdonald and Pettit, op. cit. It may be found reminiscent of the case for individualism made by F. A. Hayek in 'Scientism and the Study of Society', reprinted (with omissions) in John O'Neill, *Modes of Individualism and Collectivism*, Heinemann, London, 1973.

7 The embrace of individualism

Now that we have satisfied ourselves of the truth of ontological individualism, we may look at the implications of espousing the doctrine. Some of those implications, in a loose sense of that phrase, we have already seen. We have mentioned that being an ontological individualist gives one motivating reason for adopting that reformist attitude by which we identified individualism in the first place. Specifically, it encourages one to believe that the purpose of institutions is to serve the interests of individuals and that institutions are perfectible so far as fulfilling this purpose goes. Such reformism, which is embodied in the enterprise of political philosophy, i.e. the search for a criterion of justice, contrasts with the distinctive institutionalist attitudes: inertial, reactionary or revolutionary. What we now want to see is whether, apart from this reformist outlook, we can identify further views that follow naturally on the ontological thesis that institutions are nothing over and beyond individuals. In particular, we must examine the connections, if there are any, between individualism in this sense and other doctrines that commonly go under that name.

Individualism means many things apart from the ontological thesis, or the reformist disposition which is associated with it. In this chapter I propose to go through various theories that have been described as individualism in order to see whether the onto-logical commitment entails assuming a favourable attitude towards these. I will look first at the so-called theory of the abstract individual, something that I call developmental individualism, and at the closely associated epistemological individualism which traces all ideas and insights to personal preconception or experience. Then I will consider methodological individualism and a doctrine that sometimes also goes by that name but which I dub heuristic individualism: the first puts a constraint on hypotheses that should be taken seriously in social science, the second prescribes a strategy for the formulation of such hypotheses. Finally I will look at some normative varieties of the theory: ethical individualism, according to which each agent has to decide on what his guiding values are, and various forms of policy-making individualism – political, economic and religious. The value of the exercise will not be just that of seeing what follows from the ontological doctrine apart from a reformist attitude. It will also be of value to see what does not follow, for one of the problems with declaring oneself to be an individualist in the ontological sense is that one is often thought then to hold things which, except in name, are quite distinct views.

The theory of the abstract individual, developmental individualism, is a doctrine pilloried in the works of thinkers as various as Marx and Durkheim, F. H. Bradley and G. H. Mead. It supposes, so far as it allows of exact formulation, that the significant characteristics of human beings are determined independently of social initiation and experience. Nowadays it might be given a reading which emphasises the genetic determination of personal qualities but the classic form in which it has invited criticism ignores such argument. It depicts people as rational egoists whose selfish ends are the product of common inclination and whose strategies for satisfying those ends are the output of native cunning. The view is often thought to be implicated in Hobbes's model of the contract that inaugurates political society and in the more mundane models which economists use to explain and predict market phenomena. What it suggests is that individuals derive their goals from a psychological rather than a sociological source, and that we may expect to find common patterns of motivation and reasoning across very different cultural contexts. Such contexts do not deeply touch people, they merely provide them with different theatres of action.

It will be clear why a view of this kind is much pilloried, even in a time when significant genetic determination of individuals is widely acknowledged. If anything in social life is salient, it is the extent to which people learn from their elders and peers what it is to be happy or unhappy, successful or unsuccessful, likeable or unlikeable: even what it is to be a self, and to think the thoughts and do the things that give proof of full selfhood. Are we forced by virtue of our ontological commitment on institutions to reject the evidence of this social formation of individuals? Happily we are not. Socialisation is a process which individual people undergo at the hands of other individuals, as they are introduced to received ideas, established norms, traditional practices, and the like. If it is something that institutions can be said to effect, it remains that it is brought about through the intermediacy of people. Thus the denial that institutions are anything over and beyond individuals is no embarrassment to someone who wishes to emphasise the importance of socialisation and to push aside the perspective of developmental individualists. Ontological individualism gives no extra credibility to this particular counterpart.

Associated with the theory of the abstract individual is a view which Steven Lukes describes as epistemological individualism. This suggests that what ideas and beliefs we form are a function either of our inherited natures or of our individual experiences. On the one hand a rationalist story may be told about the role of innate preconceptions in determining our thought processes and models of the world. On the other, an empiricist account may be given of our habit of inducing general pictures from particular observations and perhaps, in existentialist tone, of our compulsion for projecting individually conceived interpretations on to the things that we confront perceptually. In either case the emphasis will be thrown off the influence of tradition, social position and ideology in moulding the cognitive disposition of the individual subject. It will appear that socialisation plays a very little part in determining how a person comes to see things and understand them.

We are no more committed to embracing this doctrine by our ontological individualism than we were the more general developmental theory. As in the other case our individualism leaves us free to decide for or against the dogma on hand. Whether the dogma is true or false is less clear in this instance than in the other although it may be mentioned that our learning machine model of theory-construction would seem to run against it. If it happens that the very acknowledgment and description of perceptual data is subject to the influence of theorising then, assuming that theory-construction is distinctively marked by the tradition in which it is pursued, it appears that the social conditioning of knowledge goes very deep indeed. Such conditioning is the effect of individual on individual and it can be readily admitted by someone who denies that institutions have an ontological autonomy.

Methodological individualism is the next doctrine on the agenda of our discussion. This, on at least one understanding of it, says that it is unlikely, if not absolutely impossible, that there are laws of social life whose obtaining we cannot explain within the humanistic conception of agents. It refuses seriously to countenance the prospect of nomic regularities, say in the succession of B-type events on A-type ones, which cannot be causally traced to the normally operative attitudes of individuals. There may be non-nomic or accidental regularities of this kind but there are hardly any which underpin counterfactuals, giving us reason to believe that the succession is not a coincidence and that if we had brought about an A just now, or at any other time, we would thereby have realised a B too. This methodological doctrine puts a significant constraint on the sorts of hypotheses that social scientists should take seriously. It suggests that any humanistically inexplicable correlation should be taken as a coincidence, short of its being so salient that to take it in that way would be to scramble our intuitions about probability.

To take a discovered correlation as nomic rather than accidental would be surprising if doing so made the reliable obtaining of the regularity seem causally miraculous; at any rate this would be surprising if the correlation were not entirely salient, being observed only in a short run of instances, or being less than universal. And yet this is what a social scientist would be doing if he construed a humanistically inexplicable correlation as a law of social life; we may assume, social science being what it is, that any correlation offered will be short-run and non-salient. So at least our ontological individualism would lead us to believe, counselling that individual agents are the only causal agents on the social scene which might support a nomic regularity, and that a humanistically inexplicable regularity must therefore be without any causal foundation. Thus it appears that to be an ontological individualist is to be attracted also to the methodological version of the doctrine. It is indeed unlikely that there are humanistically unintelligible laws of social life, if it would be surprising for a social scientist to take a humanistically inexplicable correlation as evidence of a law. A good deal more would need to be said on this matter to make the connections clear and compelling, but these remarks must do to establish at least a motivational bond between ontological and methodological individualism.

Closely related to the methodological doctrine, and often indeed confused with it, is something that I call heuristic individualism. This assumes the truth of the other view and goes further in prescribing a strategy of investigation for social science. What it says is that in doing social science we should always take our starting point from individual motives and actions. This prescription may be understood on a model familiar from economics, or on one more associated with history. On the economic way of doing things we reconstruct provisionally the beliefs and desires of typical agents in a given sort of circumstance, usually putting severe egoistic constraints on the sort of motivation allowed, and we work out, first, what the agents would rationally have done in that situation and, second, what the outcome would have been of such individual actions. Where the predictions come out right we assume that our motivational and other premises were correct and we give ourselves a way of making predictions for other similar circumstances; where they are not fulfilled, we go back and amend the premises until we succeed in getting the correct results. The historical approach is a variant on this which is appropriate when we have independent access to the people involved in the events we wish to explain and can help ourselves to collateral information on their motivation and understanding. Here we again assume that the agents acted rationally and this assumption, together with the collateral information on their beliefs and desires, enables us to reconstruct what they would do in the circumstances under discussion, and what such action would lead to at the aggregate level. This reconstruction is then tested, as it was in the other case, by whether it represents the events to be explained as an intelligible outcome. Where it does, we may rest content; where it does not, we must go back to the drawing board.

Is heuristic individualism supported by the ontological doctrine in the manner of its methodological comrade? Well, it certainly is not ruled out by that doctrine but neither, I think, does it receive distinctive encouragement from it. Consistently with thinking of institutions as nothing over and beyond individuals, we may allow that resolving the focus of our sociological scrutiny at the level of individuals can be an unproductive ploy. There is no reason to think that all the interesting and significant patterns in social life will manifest themselves at that level of attention, even though they may be all explicable there. On the old counsel of seeing the wood, not the trees, we should be prepared to explore society also at that level where our gaze is fixed on large scale entities and phenomena: nations and classes, cultures and economies, migrations and wars. It may well be that within such a perspective we shall detect regularities, albeit regularities that call for individualistic explanation, which would have eluded us had we confined our view to individual actors. It is doubtful whether the regularity connecting the introduction of money to peasants with the decline of the manorial system would have been visible to someone following strictly the counsel of heuristic individualism.

Having dealt with the developmental and epistemological, methodological and heuristic, forms of the theory, we come finally to the normative varieties of individualism. Ethical individualism is the claim that each person's ethical values, whether he realises it or not, reflect a choice or decision on his part: if they were not deliberately adopted at any point, they continue only because they are not deliberately dismissed. More important perhaps, the doctrine suggests that each individual ought to take in hand explicitly the task of sorting out his value-judgments, grounding them systematically in self-conscious decisions or in a self-conscious style. Sometimes described as ethical decisionism, it may be recognised as a common strand in R. M. Hare's prescriptivism and in the brand of existentialism represented by Sartre.

The ethical individualist is characterised by his rejection of realism in respect of values: it is because he thinks that values are not imposed by experience that he thinks they ought to be made into matters of explicit personal decision. One might reject realism and stop short of such a doctrine but it is enough for us to notice that being a realist about values would certainly prevent one taking the decisionist step. Clearly our ontological commitment on the relation between institutions and individuals leaves us free to be realist or not, and thus it gives us the possibility of rejecting ethical individualism or, presumably, of accepting it. There is no particular connection here, one way or the other.

The other normative individualisms concern policy-making rather than personal style. There are three doctrines which may be distinguished: political individualism, which would insist that government ought not to interfere with individuals except in the prevention of harm; economic individualism, which would specifically prohibit the unnecessary intervention of government in the operation of the economy; and religious individualism, which would argue, again in a more specific vein, that government ought not to curtail freedom of religious practice. The second and third doctrines are corollaries of the first, but they might either of them be defended without endorsement of that source.

Is any such policy-making individualism implicated in the ontological theory that we have espoused? As clearly as in the ethical case, it is not. It is true that our individualism encourages the reformist belief that the purpose of institutions is to serve the interests of individuals. But it suggests nothing about what those interests are and nothing therefore on what restrictions they entail for government activity. The identification of the interests, and the elaboration of the demands that they make, is the job of political philosophy. That job is made to seem plausible, but it is not pre-empted, by individualism of the ontological sort.

In conclusion, one last point. Political individualism is sometimes taken to mean not the *laissez faire* theory just characterised, but rather the social contract outlook according to which individuals may be assumed to have given their consent to any regime for which they vote in free elections, or even any regime against which they fail to revolt. This rather bizarre view does not follow, any more than its homonym, from the commitment that we have made. Even though institutions always survive through the maintenance of individual patterns of behaviour, and even though those patterns are intentionally forthcoming, it does not follow that they reflect full consent. We saw in the first chapter that practices often emerge in circumstances where some people have greater bargaining power than others and where the others, therefore, may have to make damaging compromises: this, or face the prospect of chaos. Even where there are free elections such relative powerlessness may devalue the votes cast by great numbers of people, giving them something short of the significance of full consent to the regime preferred. For it may be that those people vote for *A* over *B* when, if the option were there, they would have gone for a third form of government, *C*.

In this chapter we have charted the consequences of our commitment to ontological individualism, beyond acceptance of the reformist theses on the purpose and perfectibility of institutions. We saw that neither developmental nor epistemological individualism follows on the commitment, it being possible to allow for the effects of socialisation while denying that institutions are anything over and beyond individuals. Methodological individualism, we argued, does receive considerable support from the ontological doctrine, but this is not so for the oft associated heuristic claim: we may agree that social laws are all humanistically explicable without concluding that social science ought always to take its starting point from individuals. Finally, we saw that the ontological theory has no implications, favourable or hostile, so far as the normative versions of individualism go: it may or it may not be that right is on the side of the ethical individualist or on that of individualists in the policy-making sphere.

Bibliographical note

A useful survey of various forms of individualism is provided in Steven Lukes, *Individualism*, Blackwell, Oxford, 1973. The theory of the abstract individual may be discerned in Hobbes's *Leviathan* or in any neo-classical textbook of micro-economics. Epistemological individualism is evident in the classic works of rationalism and empiricism and, perhaps most obviously, in recent positivistic tracts: see for example, Ernest Nagel, *The Structure of Science*, Routledge & Kegan Paul, London, 1961. For an account of methodological individualism, and a development of the argument suggested here in its defence, see Graham Macdonald and Philip Pettit, *Semantics and Social Science*, Routledge & Kegan Paul, London, forthcoming. A good sourcebook of readings on the issue is John O'Neill, ed., *Modes of Individualism and Collectivism*, Heinemann, London, 1973. Heuristic individualism in sociology is particularly associated with exchange theory and a good critical introduction to this is Anthony Heath, *Rational Choice and Social Exchange*, Cambridge University Press, 1976. The doctrine of ethical individualism, as suggested in the text, pervades J. P. Sartre, *Being and Nothingness*, translated by Hazel Barnes, Methuen, London, 1957, and also R. M. Hare, *The Language of Morals*, Oxford University Press, 1952, and *Freedom and Reason*, Oxford University Press, 1963. The policy-making forms of individualism are popular doctrines particularly associated with the liberal tradition; they can be seen for example in John Stuart Mill's work, especially *On Liberty* (1859), in *Utilitarianism Liberty and Representative Government*, Dent, London, 1972.

Part III The proprietarian criterion of justice

8 Justice as legitimacy

The task of a political philosophy, as we are now well aware, is to provide a rational basis for selecting one charter or one family of charters over the other frameworks available for ordering social life. It is that of providing a criterion for determining when it is appropriate to describe a charter as just: when it is plausible to say that it is the best charter, or one of the set of best charters, from the point of view of the interests of individuals. In the remaining three parts of this text we shall examine the major candidates considered in the contemporary literature for the role of criterion of justice. They are, respectively: that a charter is just when it is legitimate, that it is just when it maximises people's welfare, and that it is just when it is fair. In this chapter we begin the scrutiny of these criteria with an initial account of the legitimacy proposal.

The notion of legitimacy supposes pre-existing standards of right and wrong, proper and improper. What is maintained in the theory of justice which we have to investigate is that a charter is just if, and only if, it meets such antecedent constraints. Its justice consists in its propriety in respect of those assumed principles. The doctrine which proposes the equation of justice with legitimacy may on this account be dubbed proprietarianism. The name will not be found particularly appealing but it serves some useful purposes of reference and it reflects a nice parallel with the other theories of justice. Where proprietarianism makes propriety or legitimacy the test of justice, welfare is given criterial status by utilitarianism and fairness by contractarianism.

The proprietarian tradition, albeit not under that name, goes back at least to the seventeenth-century theory of natural rights, receiving a classic formulation in the work of John Locke. We shall not be concerned, however, with traditional expressions of the doctrine, only with a particularly powerful contemporary statement of it. That statement is Robert Nozick's *Anarchy, State and Utopia*, henceforth referred to as ASU. It is by no means the only recent expression of proprietarian ideas but it is certainly the most robust, and probably also the most influential, document within the contemporary development of the tradition. One distinctive feature, and it gives us a further reason for concentrating on Nozick, is that it sets out a systematic view on the nature of the just society. Many proponents of the natural rights approach stop short of this, offering arguments for the existence of such rights, and perhaps giving illustrations of the demands which some of the rights make, but leaving most of the work of political assessment to the intuitions of the initiate. Indeed, were it not for Nozick, it would have been tempting to consign natural rights theory to the residual category of intuitionistic political philosophies. As characterised in chapter 4, the intuitionist is content to describe a number of values which the just charter should satisfy without specifying how those values are to be weighted against one another; what he offers is not a criterion of justice in the sense in which a scalar, serial or straightforward formula is such, but a licence for the exercise of a certain sort of intuition.

The leading proprietarian theme is that individuals have certain rights independently of the form of social organisation under which they live and that these rights put constraints on the institutional arrangements that can be made for individuals. The rights are the antecedent standards of right and wrong which were mentioned above. They define the legitimacy or propriety that a charter of social life must aspire to realise if it is to deserve of being called just. Before we follow through with the proprietarian account of such standards it will be useful to pause for a short while over the general notion of rights. What will appear is that the concept is invoked commonly in a variety of senses and that the meaning which the proprietarian gives to it is a highly distinctive one.

In order to get an idea of rights other than the proprietarian's, and one which is arguably in more common employment, let us recall the definition of a practice which we offered in the first chapter. A practice, we argued, is a regularity of behaviour to which nearly everyone in a society conforms, to which nearly everyone expects everyone else to conform, and which is such that this expectation gives nearly everyone some reason for wanting deviance discouraged, including his own deviance if that is a necessary cost of general discouragement. This concept gave us a common means of characterising the different aspects of social life, for we saw that the civil, economic and legal spheres could each be described as forms of life which resulted from people's abiding by certain practices.

With the notion of a practice in place we can introduce a corresponding concept of right. If a set of practices is established in society then certain types of behaviour, such as complaint against conformity or obstruction to conformity, will naturally be criticised: the reason each person has for wanting deviance to be discouraged will give him grounds to hold the offender blame-worthy, if he is called upon to make a judgment by the injured party. The other side of this coin is that the establishment of a set of practices also means that other types of behaviour will naturally be condoned: each person will have grounds for morally support-ing someone who acts in conformity to the practices, against complaint or obstruction. Such condoned, or at least uncriticised, forms of action may be said in a common use of the phrase to be within the rights of any party to the practices, where the other sorts of behaviour were offences against such rights.

On the concept in question here a right is the ability to perform a certain type of action without exposing oneself to criticism of a practice-based kind: it is the capacity to exercise a certain choice with institutional impunity. A right is a discretion one may exer-cise, an option one may take up, without breaking the force-lines of moral criticism which any set of practices institutes. Such an institutional impunity may come by design or default. It comes by design where the practices cover explicitly the area of behaviour at issue, as when they render legitimate a particular treatment of certain persons or employment of certain things. It comes by default where the area of behaviour is one for which none of the practices legislates: say, the exercise of choice on whether or not to clean up a public street or on whether or not to paint an unclaimed rock offshore. In the first case the practices give one ground for complaint against interference, in the second they do not: roughly speaking, one's rights in the former instance are correlated with duties on the part of others, one's rights in the latter are not. What is in common is the defining characteristic of practice-based rights, that in exercising the discretion one does not expose oneself to criticism: so far at least as the practices go, the action in question is unimpeachable.

The institutional rights which we have been envisaging happen to be reciprocal rights. They are rights which any person, insti-tutional as well as individual, can have and having them, there-fore, is matched by acknowledging them, although some may do much better than others in this process. The feature of reciprocity can be seen in someone's general rights not to be obstructed in doing this or that but it is also present in the special rights such as the promisee has against the promiser or either party to a contract has against the other. Besides reciprocal rights of this kind we often find certain recipient rights recognised in a society, such as the right of every child in the United Kingdom to a free primary and secondary education, or the right of the unemployed person to a certain support from the state. These are perfectly parallel to the others, making it possible for individuals to make the appropriate claims with impunity and making it an offence on the part of the authorities to refuse to meet the claims. The distinction between the two sorts of rights is not of great analytical significance but it is naturally sharpened by *laissez faire* theorists who are opposed to the welfare state. It is sometimes drawn, not as that between reciprocal and recipient rights, but rather in terms of negative *versus* positive rights.

The critical purpose to which rights in the institutional sense are put is that of indicting individuals or groups with a certain sort of failure to abide by the existing practice. When an individual is said to have no right to behave in the way he does, that is taken as itself a form of rebuke, not merely as a descriptive comment on the fact that the person is not conforming to the recognised regularities. It is common knowledge in a community which sustains certain practices that anyone who describes an agent as having no right to act in the way he does is unfavourably disposed towards that behaviour and, that being so, the individual making such a comment must be taken to intend that he be interpreted in the manner in question. He must be construed as saying something with an evaluative as well as a descriptive intent. Thus the concept of institutional rights comes to have a normative as well as an analytical function.

For good or ill, the institutional concept is only capable of serving a very limited sort of criticism. It enables one to castigate behaviour within a system of practices, which fails to accord appropriately with the demands that the system makes. But this criticism is entirely from within, it is essentially intrasystemic. Thus the concept of institutional rights is of no use from the point of view of someone who wants to judge, not the performance of particular parties, but the constitution of the system itself. It is this lack which has encouraged the development of an entirely different concept, and which has led people to say that individuals have rights independently of the institutions within which they exist: rights which those institutions may be criticised for failing to acknowledge or respect.

Non-institutional rights may be understood in a weaker or a stronger sense and it is only the second that introduces the proprietarian perspective, strictly understood. To take the weaker sense first, all that may be meant by saying that individuals have certain rights independently of institutions is that there are considerations about human beings which give reason why practices should be organised in one way rather than another. In this sense the assertion of such rights amounts simply to the denial of the legal positivist viewpoint that there is no higher court of appeal than that which the existing institutional pattern offers. It is a rejection of any picture of human beings which represents them as morally malleable, amenable to just any system of social organisation. What it emphasises is that human beings are not putty in the hands of institutions: human beings, and the phrase comes in a natural rhetorical turn, have rights against institutions as well as rights within them.

To allow such talk of rights is not yet to endorse the proprietarian philosophy, for what is said can be given a perfectly feasible interpretation within a utilitarian or contractarian point of view. On such a construal, the ascription of a non-institutional right to an individual comes to the claim that any practices which do not establish the corresponding institutional discretion are subject to negative criticism: a criticism that may be grounded in any conception of justice. On this approach it can be argued that literally rights continue to be understood in the institutional sense and that the new usage is a non-literal extension of the concept. If a person is said to have a certain right r in the literal sense, that means that he is able to exercise the corresponding discretion with institutional impunity. If he is said to have the right r in the extended sense, the society being one where the required discretion is not in fact accorded to him, that means that the society is inferior on some favoured criterion of justice to the society where r is an institutional right and other things are equal.

The weak sense of non-institutional rights is probably that which is at issue in recent documents such as the *United Nations Declaration of Human Rights*, even though the rhetoric is consciously modelled on eighteenth-century pronouncements of a more proprietarian stamp: for example, the *Virginian Declaration of Rights* of 1776, or the *Declaration of the Rights of Man and of Citizens* promulgated by the French National Assembly in 1789. One reason for thinking this is that many of the rights mentioned in recent documents are of a recipient kind, such as the rights to material necessities and to free education, and these are rather more easily vindicated if they are understood in the weak sense. The usual basis on which the right to free education is defended is utilitarian, or perhaps egalitarian: it is said that people are happier in a society where they all have educational facilities, this being a source of satisfaction to each and also an insurance that

the talents of the society are properly tapped. People have a right
to free education, then, in the extended sense that a society which
does not institutionalise the right is inferior on the utilitarian
standard to a society which does, assuming that other things are
equal.

But we must come now to the stronger, literal reading which a
proprietarian philosophy gives to the concept of non-institutional
rights. On this interpretation, it is not just that there are certain
considerations about people which give reason why practices
should be organised in one way rather than another. More specifically, the considerations assume the form of fundamental constraints on how an individual may be treated without his consent
by other individuals and groups, in particular by the state. To
speak of natural rights on this view is not a rhetorical conceit. It
is to refer to matters that are held to present themselves for
consideration to anyone who has an understanding of what it is to
be a human being. Where institutional rights are perfectly real
entities in the world of social organisation, these natural rights are
taken to be just as real a part of the world untouched by human
artifice. They are matters for factual scrutiny, albeit they are
usually invoked in terms which have an evaluative connotation,
as when we say that such and such treatment is wrong, that it
ought not to happen, or just that it is contrary to someone's rights.

The characterisation of the rights countenanced by the proprietarian may take the form of a list, as when it is said that people
have the right to life, liberty and property, or it may be provided
by means of a set of injunctions, prescribing some acts and for-
bidding others. A third, and more traditional, way of presenting
them, however, is to describe a situation where people have not
consented to any mutually accommodating compromise of the
rights and where the rights are institutionally established, being
respected in the general practice of individuals. Such a situation
is described, in the received phrase, as a state of nature, since it
is a dispensation within which no formal political authority has
been instituted.

The rights which Robert Nozick makes into the foundation of
his political philosophy are very much in line with the rights
recognised by John Locke and his fullest presentation of these
consists in a reminder, with quotations, of the dispensation in
Locke's state of nature. The passage is worth quoting in full.

> Individuals in Locke's state of nature are in 'a state of
> perfect freedom to order their actions and dispose of their
> possessions and persons as they think fit, within the
> bounds of the law of nature, without asking leave or

dependency upon the will of any other man'. The bounds
of the law of nature require that 'no one ought to harm
another in his life, health, liberty, or possessions'. Some
persons transgress these bounds, 'invading others' rights
and . . . doing hurt to one another', and in response
people may defend themselves or others against such
invaders of rights. The injured party and his agents may
recover from the offender 'so much as may make
satisfaction for the harm he has suffered'; 'everyone has a
right to punish the transgressors of that law to such a
degree as may hinder its violation'; each person may, and
may only 'retribute to (a criminal) so far as calm reason
and conscience dictate, what is proportionate to his
transgression, which is so much as may serve for
reparation and restraint'. (ASU, p. 10)

Such natural rights as are indicated here serve for a proprietarian like Nozick as fundamental constraints on how people may be
treated without their consent, subject to one qualification mentioned below. What makes the constraints fundamental is that
they are not compelling on the ground of bringing about any
further good. They contrast with the conditions which a utilitarian
might want to impose in the name of human welfare, or a contractarian in the name of fairness. If any justification is to be given
for them it will be in terms of the conception of the human agent
which they express, not by reference to an end which fulfilling
them promotes. What makes them constraints on the other hand,
rather than objectives or goals, is that transgressing one cannot
be justified by reference to the consequences thereby achieved,
even the consequence of reducing the total amount of transgression that takes place. With an objective such as lessening pain one
is naturally justified in offending against the objective in a course
of action so long as doing so means that the objective will be the
more fully realised in the end: you may cause a person or a group
of persons greater pain than they experienced before your intervention so long as you will thereby ensure lesser pain in the long
term than they would otherwise have undergone. With a constraint this sort of trade-off is forbidden; one's breaking the constraint has a negative infinite weight which cannot be outbalanced
by the weight attaching to the prevention of more widespread
transgression.

There is one qualification made by Nozick to the proprietarian
claim that natural rights are fundamental constraints on how
people may be treated without their consent. In order to see how
he can contemplate the qualification it is necessary first to recog-

nise that once compensation has been paid for a transgression then arguably the wrong has been put right. This means that there is a *prima facie* case for allowing transgression of a natural right provided that it is followed by compensation. Nozick does not think that transgression should be tolerated whenever it is understood that compensation will be paid: this, for reasons that will be mentioned in the chapter after next. However, he is prepared to allow transgression-cum-compensation in one particular sort of case and here we have a qualification on the universal prescription of respect for natural rights. The case arises when someone's behaving within his rights is liable to cause others harm, so that there is a risk that it will not after all be legitimate, and where those others cannot for one reason or another get the agent's consent for their preventing him from behaving in that way.

An example of this case might be that of an epileptic's driving an automobile, where there is a risk that he will cause harm to others but where, we suppose, his consent to being prevented from driving cannot be secured. In such a case Nozick argues that transgression-cum-compensation is justified, that the community may legitimately stop the epileptic driving so long as it compensates him by providing free public transport or some measure of the sort. He characterises the case as one where the trespasser (the community) receives no positive benefit from trespassing but merely prevents some harm being done, and where the victim (the epileptic) is disadvantaged by the trespass, not merely prevented from bettering his lot in some way. The details of this characterisation reflect a desire to limit the case so as to match our intuitions about when someone may be legitimately restrained in the manner in question. Nozick does not think that he has worked out the details adequately but we need not concern ourselves with them in any case. All that it is important to recognise is that while natural rights generally serve as fundamental constraints on how people may be treated without their consent, transgression followed by compensation is sometimes regarded as legitimate by the proprietarian.

This will do as an initial introduction to the perspective of the proprietarian tradition, and specifically to the point of view represented by Robert Nozick. We have seen that our account of social life allows us to define a concept of institutional rights but that this is only of normative use in criticising the behaviour of parties within a system, not in castigating the performance of the system itself. The concept can be extended to allow for the criticism of systems, people being said to have, not just those rights actually recognised within an existing set of practices, but also whatever rights would be acknowledged within the system that is regarded as just on some independent criterion: say, a utilitarian or contractarian one. The proprietarian tradition goes further even than making this extension. It suggests that people have natural rights, i.e. rights which do not presuppose the existence of institutions, in a more literal sense than the extension allows. These rights are thought to offer themselves to the intuition of anyone who thinks about what it is to be a human being. They are represented as constraints on how individuals may be treated without their consent, constraints which cannot legitimately be broken except in certain limited cases where transgression is followed by compensation. And they are said to be fundamental constraints, since they do not derive their justification from any end-state which fidelity to them might promote. By way of characterising those that he recognises, Robert Nozick refers us to Locke's state of nature. This is that social situation within which natural rights are institutionalised, the practice being to recognise them, but where people have not consented to any diminution of their individual rights such as might be thought to secure greater mutual accommodation. The rights that stand out in this characterisation are the right to do as one wishes, in particular to dispose as one likes of one's property, short of causing harm to others, and the right to punish those who offend against that primary right in one's own case, within the limit dictated by 'calm reason and conscience'.

Bibliographical note

Clearly, the major source for this chapter is Robert Nozick, *Anarchy, State and Utopia*, Blackwell, Oxford, 1974. This, as mentioned in the text, is the outstanding recent statement of proprietarian ideas. Locke's ideas on rights, and they are clearly important to Nozick, can be found in his *Two Treatises of Government*, ed. Peter Laslett, Cambridge University Press, 1963. The history of the concept of rights up to Locke is traced in Richard Tuck, *Natural Rights Theories*, Cambridge University Press, 1979. For the eighteenth-century revolutionary documents, which incorporate proprietarian notions, see D. G. Ritchie, *Natural Rights*, Allen & Unwin, London, 1894. Some recent discussions of rights, institutional as well as natural, are collected in A. I. Melden, ed., *Human Rights*, Wadsworth, Belmont, California, 1970, and Eugene Kamenka and Alice Erh-Soon Tay, eds, *Human Rights*, Edward Arnold, London, 1978. The texts of important contemporary declarations of rights, declarations which are not usually proprietarian in tone, are contained in Maurice Cranston, *What are Human Rights?*, Bodley Head, London, 1973. A recent defence of a rights-based political philosophy, although again it is not particularly proprietarian, is Norman E. Bowie and Robert L. Simon, *The Individual and the Political Order*, Prentice-Hall, Englewood Cliffs, NJ. 1977. For an account of rights as constraints, which ties up quite well with Nozick's, see Ronald Dworkin, *Taking Rights Seriously*, Duckworth, London, 1978, chapters 4 and 7. Dworkin espouses a criterion of justice which puts proprietarian constraints on a utilitarian standard.

9 *The dictates of legitimacy*

The proprietarian rights such as Nozick recognises give a criterion by which social charters may be assessed. Any charter which violates those constraints must be objectionable, and any charter which satisfies them just. And what sorts of arrangements are liable to fail this test? Here there is a problem. It appears that any regime beyond a dispensation like Locke's state of nature is bound to offend against people's natural rights. Any such state will involve taxation, if only to fulfil the most minimal functions, and taxation means interfering with the right of individuals to dispose as they wish of their possessions. And even if its expenses are met from elsewhere, a regime of the kind envisaged must have the power in other respects to coerce people against their presumed will: to stop them, for example, from taking the exaction of punishment into their own hands; otherwise it will not mark a significant break with the state of nature. How then can the proprietarian stop short of the unfetching conclusion that the only just ordering of social life is a relatively anarchistic one such as that which is represented in Locke's state of nature?

This problem has been one of the leading themes within the natural rights tradition and it has received a variety of answers. The approaches have generally argued that one or another non-anarchistic regime is justified in so far as the people living under it may be presumed to have given their consent to the forceful behaviour of the state in their regard. This appeal to tacit consent, and perhaps to a founding social contract, is scarcely persuasive; it can be turned to whatever purpose attracts the political philosopher and any instance of it is bound to smack of rationalisation. Nor does there seem to be much hope of invoking the compensation principle mentioned in the last chapter to justify non-anarchistic arrangements. Just as it is implausible to invoke people's tacit consent to any forceful treatment which they receive at the hands of a given regime, so it is uncompelling to argue that in every such instance there is an appropriate form of compensation offered to the person who is roughly handled. Like tacit consent, indirect compensation would seem to offer an instrument of justification that is too powerful for proprietarian comfort.

It is to Robert Nozick's credit that he has devised an entirely original solution to this problem and has given grounds for believing that the strictest proprietarian can espouse a form of social organisation tighter than that which Locke's state of nature represents. He argues that if it can be shown that such a state of nature naturally gives rise to a regime of a different sort, and does this without involving the infringement of natural rights, then it is reasonable for the proprietarian to cherish the second sort of order above the first. The second form of organisation is just as satisfying as the first since it comes about without the transgression of any natural rights and it has the extra merit of coming about, not only when it is instituted in its own name, but also when the other order is established in its stead. Nozick's claim is irresistible and it only remains for him to show that there is some charter of social life which automatically, and morally, takes the place of a Lockean state of nature.

The dispensation which he thinks would replace anarchy in the appropriate fashion is what he calls the minimal state. This a regime which is extremely liberal in civil life, and extremely non-socialist in economic. Whether it is fully democratic is a moot point but its judiciary is certainly assumed to make its decisions fairly. Nozick argues that such a minimal state will naturally issue from any state of nature, and will do this without trespassing on anyone's natural rights. The argument is a derivation of the minimal state from the anarchistic situation: if you like, a *reductio ad politicum* of the legally unstructured social order. Two conditions are put on the derivation. The first is that it represents the minimal state as coming about under the pressure of rational self-interest, without anyone's having to form the conception of such a state in order for the process to be consummated. This condition stipulates that the minimal state must issue from an invisible hand process such as classical economists often invoke. The point of it is that it offers a reasonable interpretation of what it is for such a state to arise automatically: nothing would seem more natural to expect than a social outcome to which people will be driven by rational self-interest, whether or not they have the wit to see where they are going. The second condition on the derivation is that is depicts the minimal state as emerging without the infringement of anyone's natural rights. Where the first guarantees that the emergence is automatic, or at least as automatic as can be expected, this ensures that it is a morally unobjectionable process. Only if the minimal state has a perfectly unimpeachable pedigree will it command the affections of the proprietarian, as distinct merely from causing him to become resigned to it.

The emergence of the state is described informally by Nozick but we may usefully divide it into stages. There are four of these and I will provide a sketch of them in chronological order.

1 In face of the inconveniences of the state of nature individuals form or join protection agencies (ASU, pp. 12–15). Nozick supposes that in the state of nature each individual will naturally form a mutual protection association with his family and friends, calling on them in his own defence and allowing himself to be called on in theirs. Such an association, he argues, would be inconvenient, involving everyone in the use of arms, and leaving each group at the mercy of the chronic complainer; also it would give rise to difficulty in the case of differences within the group. It is inevitable – and here we see rational self-interest in operation – that any such association should give way to a protection agency which, for a fee, would arbitrate all complaints made by its members and, where appropriate, act in retaliation against offenders, those within the agency as well as those outside.

2 One such agency, or a federation of agencies, becomes dominant in each area (ASU, pp. 15–17). There are three possibilities, according to Nozick: in a given area one agency wins all the battles, one agency wins in one part of the area, another in a second, two agencies fight evenly and often, neither attaining supremacy anywhere. In the first case, the winning agency will naturally become dominant, people in the area having the choice of joining it or not joining an agency at all. In the second, the area will split, people towards one end joining one agency, people towards the other joining the opposing agency, and a borderland getting established in between. In the third case, the two agencies, rather than fight each other recurrently, will cut their costs and agree to accept a third judgment on every difference between them, thus forming a dominant federation of agencies. In each of these cases the outcome described is inevitable because of the operation of rational self-interest.

Have we already reached the state in our derivation? A dominant protection agency, as Nozick admits, looks very like a minimal state. 'Out of anarchy, pressed by spontaneous groupings, mutual protection associations, division of labour, market pressures, economies of scale, and rational self-interest there arises something very much resembling a minimal state or a group of geographically distinct minimal states' (ASU, pp. 16–17).

There are two features, Nozick says, which distinguish the minimal state proper from a dominant protection agency. He conceives of this state as 'the night-watchman state of classical liberal theory, limited to the functions of protecting all its citizens against violence, theft, and fraud, and to the enforcement of contracts, and so on' (ASU, p. 26). Such a state differs from a dominant protection agency, first, in claiming a certain monopoly of force and, second, in extending its protection to all citizens. As described so far there seems to be no reason why the agency should claim a monopoly of force: presumably the independents who do not join up retain the right to act on their own behalf. And neither does there seem to be reason why it should extend its protection to people other than its members: since independents do not pay they cannot expect to be protected.

The remaining stages in Nozick's derivation of the state are intended to show that rational self-interest would lead the dominant agency in any area to assume the full powers of the minimal state, and this without infringing the rights of any individual. At this point the morality condition on the emergence of the state becomes as important as the rationality one.

3 The dominant protection agency may, and will, protect its clients against the enforcement of their rights by independents, when it judges the procedures of enforcement unreliable or unfair (ASU, pp. 101–8). The reason it may do so, according to Nozick, is that each person has a right to protect himself, or to get his agency to protect him, against the sort of risk involved in independents enforcing their own rights: this, by parallel with the right of the community in our earlier example to protect itself against the risk of an epileptic's having a seizure while driving. The reason the agency will protect its client against independents in this way is that when protection agencies first appear in an area that agency will win which offers the best policy (ASU, p. 114). In offering such protection, Nozick says, a dominant agency will in effect be claiming, or at least exercising, a monopoly of force. True, the agency must allow independents to enforce their rights against its members so long as the independents follow approved procedures; and, apparently, it must allow independents to enforce their rights against each other, regardless of what procedures they follow. But still, such uses of force being supervised or restricted, Nozick has no doubt but that we must attribute a monopoly to the protection agency. It seems little enough to grant him.

4 The dominant protection agency must compensate independents for the disadvantage at which they are put, by extending its protection to them (ASU, pp. 110–11). The reason the agency must offer this compensation is that the protection of its clients against the enforcement of their rights by independents constitutes

a transgression of the rights of independents and demands to be rectified, by parallel with the compensation required in the case of the ban on epileptic drivers. The compensation will take the form of extending protection to the independents because it would be more expensive to leave them unprotected and retaliate on their behalf for each unjustified attack by a member of the agency (ASU, p. 111). A difficulty which should be mentioned here is this. Why should the agency have to compensate independents if it is the case, not that it prevents them outright from enforcing their rights, but only that it insists on certain procedures of enforcement being followed? Nozick admits, perhaps incautiously, that such may be the case. 'There will be a strong tendency for it to deem all other procedures (than its own), or even the "same" procedures run by others, either unreliable or unfair. But we need not suppose it excludes every other procedure' (ASU, p. 108).

This completes the derivation of the minimal state, for the dominant protection agency is now held to claim a certain monopoly of force and to extend its protection to all those living within its sphere. The import of the derivation is that there is one form of social organisation which the proprietarian ought to prefer to the Lockean state of nature: it is the inevitable outcome of the state of nature, and it is equally satisfactory on the count of respecting people's natural rights. If we grant the validity of the deduction, then it seems that the proprietarian criterion of justice does, after all, select a plausible charter of social life: or at least a charter which has greater plausibility than the formula for a Lockean anarchy. Further examination of the derivation can be postponed until the next, critical chapter.

At this point in the argument it might be in place to consider what Nozick has to say in fuller characterisation of his minimal state: in the last chapter of his book he seeks to represent this state in a more utopian guise than it may have seemed up to now to merit. It is not our policy, however, to follow philosophies through to the detail of the charters that they select. Instead, what we shall examine in the remainder of this chapter is a query that will inevitably be raised for someone in Nozick's position. The query is whether we might not be able to provide a proprietarian justification for a more than minimal state of precisely the kind that has been produced for the *laissez faire* dispensation. May there not be further depths in the magician's hat from which the minimal state has been drawn, depths in which less libertarian regimes may be lurking?

Nozick does not think that an appropriate derivation can be given for the more than minimal state. His reason, basically, is that he sees the distance between the anarchistic dispensation and this state as much greater than the distance between that dispensation and the minimal regime. What makes for the greater distance is that in the stricter form of organisation constant interference with people's rights is required, while in the less strict one individuals are generally allowed still to go their own way. A more than minimal state, at its best, is a redistributive regime in which people are taxed, not just in order that the authorities may be able to protect them, but also in order that they can supply various non-marketed goods, help out those in need and perhaps take over the running of certain industries; the list will be familiar from chapter 2 above. Any regime of this kind is premised on a picture of how things ought ideally to be distributed; it is unwilling to allow history to take its natural course in the allocation of goods, even a history in which no one's rights are transgressed. In a phrase of Nozick's, it operates with a patterned principle or ideal, according to which the distribution of goods ought to be determined by merit, or need, or desire, or some such non-historical consideration. The distance between the Lockean state of nature and the more than minimal regime comes of the fact that implementing any such ideal pattern requires a continuous interference with people's natural rights.

In order that we may see this, Nozick asks us to consider the case of a basketball player who is such an attraction that people are willing to pay a special extra fee to attend any game in which he is playing; the fee goes directly to him. The outcome is that at the end of the season the star player is very rich indeed, a fact which will attract the attentions of the inland revenue authorities in any redistributive regime. Let us suppose that at the beginning of the season the distribution of holdings in the society was just. In the course of the season one individual, our basketball player, earns a small fortune in perfectly righteous exchange; everyone who sees him play feels that he gets value for money. And yet the outcome at the end of the season is one which the state authorities judge to be unjust and to require rectification through taxation of the sports personality. The point which this illustrates, Nozick says, is that any ideal pattern, such as the distribution at the opening of the season, can be upset by the free transactions of people and that if it is to be maintained continuous monitoring and interference is demanded. At the limit indeed such transactions might have to be eliminated altogether. 'The socialist state would have to forbid capitalist acts between consenting adults' (ASU, p. 113).

The distance between the Lockean state of nature and the minimal regime is comparatively a very short one because in this regime there is no distributional pattern which the authorities are committed to realising. Here, as Nozick describes the dispensation, distribution is determined by a historical principle, rather than a structural or patterned one. A distribution is just if it is the result of a history of just acquisition and transfer, or if it comes of a history in which the effects of any injustice of acquisition or transfer have been rectified. Leaving aside the matter of how justice in acquisition and transfer is established, we can see that the historical ideal described does not require the sort of adjustment demanded by a structural principle. Given a just distribution as starting point then so long as people exchange goods in a just manner, not deceiving or defrauding one another for example, there will be no need for the minimal state to interfere with the resulting allocation. Precisely the opposite is true, however, in the more than minimal state, where an historical ideal of distribution is replaced by a structural one. The minimal dispensation is committed to respecting historical entitlement, the more than minimal counterpart to regarding some structural exigency: say, the demand for equality of opportunity or equality of reward. Where entitlements can be protected simply by the prevention of injustice among persons, exigencies demand a more intensive servicing and require in particular some interference with the results of just interpersonal transactions.

Where the distance between the state of nature and the minimal state is short enough to allow the appropriate derivation of the second from the first, Nozick thinks that the distance between anarchy and the more than minimal regime is too great to make such a derivation possible. In conclusion, however, it may be remarked that he is not shy of considering that possibility in some greater detail. He actually constructs an account of how people might have come to endorse a redistributive state, an account in which he tries to meet the twin conditions that the emergence described is an invisible hand process and does not involve the infringement of people's rights. On this whimsical account individuals begin the process by each agreeing to cede certain rights of control over aspects of their own behaviour in return for a reciprocal control over the behaviour of others, and they bring it to consummation by each investing all their rights over themselves in a corporation in which they are voting members. This corporation owns everybody, in the sense that it can decide anything for each person, subject to constraints of even-handedness. On the other hand each person is an equal voting member of the corporation so that, in a sense, everybody owns everybody. The regime is not so much a democracy, government of the people by the people, as 'demoktesis': ownership of the people by the people.

The demoktetic dispensation is close enough to the more than minimal state to serve the purpose of the derivation; Nozick would hope, I suspect, that it is too close for comfort. But does the derivation succeed? Does it manage to fulfil the two conditions of rational motivation and moral irreproachability? Nozick thinks that it does not. The problem is that it will always be rational for some individuals to want to opt out of the corporation in favour of a life as independents and there is no morally acceptable way in which the corporation can be sure of commanding their continuing allegiance. The best hope for the corporation would be to try to win over aspiring independents by organising a boycott against them among its members but even this is not very promising.

> It is highly unlikely that in a society containing many persons, an actual boycott such as the one described could be maintained successfully. There would be many persons opposed to the additional apparatus who could find enough others to deal with, establish a protective agency with, and so on, so as to withstand the boycott in an independent enclave (not necessarily geographical); furthermore, they could offer incentives to some participants in the boycott to break it (perhaps secretly, to avoid the response of the others who continue to maintain it). The boycott would fail, with more leaving it as they see others doing so and profiting by it. (ASU, pp. 292–93)

In this chapter we have seen how the proprietarian criterion, consisting in the assertion of certain natural rights, can be made to do useful work, selecting a charter of social life more plausible than the formula for the Lockean state of nature. The idea, devised by Robert Nozick, is that a charter is just if it would naturally come to be espoused within the state of nature, and if its espousal would not involve the violation of anyone's rights: this, rather than the more traditional but less compelling idea, that any charter is justified which can be assumed because of its virtues to have the tacit consent of citizens. Nozick claims that when put into operation in this way the proprietarian criterion turns out to justify the minimal state associated with classical liberal theory, but nothing stronger. The claim is not unconvincing. Where there is some ground for holding that the minimal state allows of being derived in the appropriate fashion from the state of nature, it seems that any derivation of its counterpart is bound to fail. The more than minimal state, as Nozick shows, is committed to a structural rather than an historical ideal of distribution and licenses so much interference with the outcomes of transactions between people, even just transactions, that no derivation seems likely. This is borne out by the failure of the derivation of the demoktetic regime to meet the appropriate conditions: it does not succeed in describing a process that is at once morally irreproachable and the work of an invisible hand.

Bibliographical note

The classic attempts to justify political charters on a proprietarian basis are found in the work of the English seventeenth-century thinkers, Thomas Hobbes and John Locke, and in that of the eighteenth-century French philosopher, Jean-Jacques Rousseau, and his Scottish contemporary, David Hume. Some relevant texts are collected in *The Social Contract*, ed. Ernest Barker, Oxford University Press, 1947. Nozick's derivation of the minimal state is provided in Part I of ASU; my analysis originally appeared in a review of the book in *Theory and Decision*, Vol. 8, 1977, and I am grateful to the editors and publishers for permission to reproduce parts of it. The account of the patterned nature of more than minimal political ideals is given in chapter 7 of Part II, and the derivation of the demoktetic dispensation in chapter 9 of the same part. At the end of chapter 9, Nozick has some very obscure remarks on what is likely to be established by devising hypothetical just histories. Since these are obscure, and since he himself says that they are tentative, I have ignored them in my presentation. A useful analysis of invisible hand derivations is given in Edna Ullman-Margalit, 'Invisible Hand Explanations', *Synthese*, vol. 39, 1978. For another defence of minimalist views see the work of F. A. Hayek, most recently *Law, Legislation and Liberty*, vol. 2, *The Mirage of Social Justice*, Routledge & Kegan Paul, London, 1976.

10 Legitimacy under analysis

We are now in a position to consider the merits of our first candidate for the role of criterion of justice. We have to inquire whether we should really be impressed by the proprietarian claim that what justice in a social charter means is that the demands of legitimacy are satisfied by that dispensation: the charter fully respects people's natural rights itself or it is the rational-cum-moral descendant of one that does so. With this criterion of justice, as with any other, there are a number of lines of investigation which we have to pursue. We must ask, first, whether it is satisfactory in its internal organisation; second, whether it can be usefully put into operation in the assessment of particular regimes; and, third, whether it meets the test of reflective equilibrium in its normative output. If it is faulty in respect of organisation or operation then we are given no reason to espouse it as a general theory which systematises our particular intuitions about justice. If it is flawed in regard to output then we may conclude not just that it fails to systematise those intuitions, but that it ignores or distorts them: what it picks out as justice is not the justice that we intuitively recognise and respond to.

Under the first heading of internal organisation there are three complaints that I wish to raise with the proprietarian criterion. My basic misgiving is that the notion of a natural right becomes unanalysable on the approach proposed. With the institutional right discussed in the chapter before last we can give conditions which are necessary and sufficient for the right to exist. A person has an institutional right to behave in a certain way if and only if the relevant practices do not give ground for complaint against the behaviour in question. No such analysis can be provided, however, for what it is to have a natural right, at least when natural right is understood in the strict proprietarian sense. We can say that someone has such a right if and only if it is always wrong, the compensation cases apart, to obstruct the relevant behaviour of the agent without his consent. But this is of little help, and scarcely passes as an analysis, since the notion of moral wrong invoked in the definition belongs to the same family of concepts as the notion requiring clarification. That problem does not arise with our account of an institutional right for we understand what it is for someone to complain, and to have an institutional ground for complaining, independently of grasping the notion under analysis. The matter is not cut and dried, since conceptual closeness is measured only in rough degrees, but it is none the less clear for that.

It is not a knockdown objection to the proprietarian idea of a natural right that it is not appropriately analysable; some notions in any theory are bound to resist analysis in the sense in question. What is suspicious, however, is that the invocation of such a right, although it is held to be *sui generis* and irreducible, is so similar to the non-literal assertion of an institutional right, an assertion that can be analysed perfectly convincingly on the lines sketched earlier. The suspicion raised is that natural rights enthusiasts are guilty of inappropriately literalising a metaphorical mode of discourse and that the non-institutional rights to which they pay homage are the product of conceptual reification. We all of us speak without misgiving of rights which certain systems fail to recognise and it must be exceedingly tempting to construe this sort of utterance literally rather than take it as a way of presenting the systems as inferior to counterparts that institutionalise the rights in question. The suspicion here is that the proprietarian has not succeeded in resisting that temptation.

A second complaint in respect of the internal organisation of the proprietarian criterion of justice is closely related to this first. Because a theorist like Nozick is unable to give an illuminating account of what it is to have a natural right, he also fails to provide any useful instructions on how to recognise a right. What exactly are the rights which may not be transgressed without the consent of the agent, exception being made for the cases where compensation is appropriate? Nozick does not answer this question for us, preferring to direct us towards the not always unambiguous remarks of Locke. More important, however, he does not give us a method for determining whether or not something is a right. It appears that we can only rely on our own intuitions and intimations. This is scarcely a satisfactory state of affairs and it constitutes a major weakness in Nozick's case for legitimacy.

The fault, it may be mentioned, does not look easy of remedy. The proprietarian, because he represents natural rights as being fundamental constraints on action, cuts off the possibility of deriving them from some further basis such as welfare or fairness. Thus the appeal to intuition seems to be required in every individual case. One exception is provided by Nozick in the case of the right of each individual not to be sacrificed for the benefit of another. He argues as follows: that morality prescribes constraints which, unlike objectives, cannot be infringed in one instance for the sake of achieving their greater realisation in others; that the best explanation for this is that individuals are separate existences, unlike the different selves that I am in the course of my life; and that the separateness of individuals ensures the right of each not to be sacrificed without his consent for the benefit of another (ASU, p. 34). Such an argument for a natural right is not forthcoming in the general case and so we are mostly forced back on intuitions.

Against the brunt of this criticism, however, it may be suggested that the ultimate test for any criterion of justice is its fit with our more or less particular judgments of justice and that the proprietarian may argue on the ground of such a fit for one or another inventory of natural rights: that inventory will be most convincing which best achieves reflective equilibrium with those judgments. This thought generates a useful insight. If the proprietarian were to rely solely on fit with particular judgments in deciding which rights to countenance, and if he were to eschew the appeal to intuition on the question of whether individuals have one or another right, then his theory might generalise his particular judgments of justice, but it would not ground them. Rights would not have to be taken as realities, and ascribing them to individuals would be seen simply as a way of proclaiming certain actions to be wrong: an activity involving nothing more than the generalisation of particular judgments of justice. This outcome, however, would be anathema to the proprietarian, for he means his natural rights to be taken seriously and to appear as the authority for the proscriptions with which they are correlated. Thus he cannot appeal solely to fit with particular judgments of justice in defence of one or another inventory of rights. He must be able to argue individually for each right in the inventory, or, and the problem is that this will be too common, he must be able to appeal to our intuition that it is indeed a right deserving of respect.

There is a third complaint to be voiced in regard to the internal organisation of the proprietarian criterion of justice. Even if we are happy with unanalysable natural rights, and do not baulk at having to appeal to intuition in evidence of them, we may yet worry that the proprietarian is not guided solely by such rights in his assessment of competing social charters. It is tempting to see in the high-minded invocation of objective rights a not uncompelling but covert appeal to factors such as the welfare of people in the society. The temptation returns us to a reading of natural rights as reifications that come of treating literally the ascription of institutional rights, in an extended sense, to individuals. Its source is the powerful feeling that whereas something like the welfare of individuals has a natural motivational force, there is little to command our affection in the metaphysical idols of the proprietarian.

This complaint gains concrete edge from the fact that at one or two places it appears that Nozick is guided as much by considerations of social prudence as he is by the demands of natural rights. Thus he argues that the transgression of rights followed by compensation is not justified in every case because to allow people to transgress so long as they compensate would be to induce fear in anyone who is liable to be a victim: knowledge that compensation will be forthcoming, even generous compensation, may not be enough to still the apprehensiveness of the potential sufferer (ASU, pp. 65–71). And why not forbid every sort of transgression-cum-compensation then? At this point the argument again takes a prudential turn, for Nozick shies away from that policy in view of the social losses that it would occasion. 'The reason one sometimes would wish to allow boundary crossings with compensation (when prior identification of the victim or communication with him is impossible) is presumably the great benefits of the act; it is worthwhile, ought to be done, and can pay its way' (ASU, p. 72). It may be possible to read such arguments in a fashion which matches the style of proprietarianism but they suggest that ultimately welfare matters as much to someone who adopts that philosophy as the rights which he so loudly proclaims.

A second instance where Nozick seems to be moved by prudential considerations is in his discussion of what he calls the Lockean proviso on acquisition. This proviso, on Nozick's version, goes as follows: 'A process normally giving rise to a permanent bequeathable property right in a previously unowned thing will not do so if the position of others no longer at liberty to use the thing is thereby worsened' (ASU, p. 178). As in the other case this proviso can be construed in a more or less proprietarian spirit, say as a principle for regulating conflicts between the right of someone to dispose as he wishes of anything that he acquires by a certain process and the rights of others to make use of previously unowned things on which they have a certain dependence. It is more natural, however, to see the invocation of the proviso as a way of ensuring that strict respect for the rights of individuals will not have a social result which is intolerable from the point of view of the welfare of individuals.

We have been through three complaints about the proprietarian criterion, which bear on its internal organisation: they are, respectively, that natural rights are made unanalysable by the proprietarian, that no method is provided whereby it can be determined whether or not something is a natural right, and that in any case the proprietarian seems to be concerned as often with welfare and the like as he is with the constraints that he explicitly avows. The second count on which any criterion of justice calls to be examined is that of whether it can be put usefully into operation in the assessment of social charters. The question is whether it provides a workable test of justice, an applicable measure of what is politically desirable.

The derivation procedure is Nozick's way of applying the proprietarian criterion to the purpose of selecting a charter: specifically, to that of presenting the minimal state as the socially desirable one. Does this procedure work? Well, as we acknowledged in the last chapter, it does seem that if the minimal state comes about more or less automatically from the situation of Lockean anarchy in which natural rights are institutionalised, and comes about without the violation of any of those natural rights, it must be regarded as superior to the dispensation from which it originates. And is Nozick's use of the procedure in the derivation of the minimal state convincing? Leaving aside the smaller criticisms which we suggested in the presentation of the argument, we may concentrate here on one particular worry. The procedure requires that the minimal state emerge by an invisible hand process and that the emergence turn out to be morally irreproachable. The worry is that whereas this picture makes rational self-interest the motivating force within the process and moral irreproachability a fortunate side-effect, Nozick at the fourth stage in his derivation puts morality in the place of rationality, predicting that the dominant protection agency will compensate independents, not because this is rationally required, but because it is morally righteous.

This subtle switch in the argument detracts seriously from the impact of Nozick's derivation, for it means that the minimal state does not appear so automatically after all. The derivation can be saved only if the assumption is made, not just that self-interest motivates people, but also that moral considerations do so. With characteristic candour Nozick admits this weakness in his argument, although the admission comes almost as an afterthought.

> We have assumed that people will generally do what they are morally required to do. . . . But one would feel more confidence if an explanation of how a state *would* arise

from a state of nature . . . specified incentives for
providing the compensation or the causes of its being
provided in addition to people's desire to do what they
ought. (ASU, p. 119)

There is also a second respect in which Nozick's derivation of
the minimal state slips moral irreproachability into a motivational
role, thus weakening the impact of the argument. At the point
where it becomes clear that independents do almost as well as
clients under the regime of the protection agency, being offered
the agency's protection against aggressors, rational self-interest
would seem to counsel any individual client that he should cease
to pay his contribution, claim the status of an independent, and
command the protection of the agency for nothing. Only the
desire to maintain the original contract with the agency, and it is
not even certain that maintenance is morally required, would seem
to prevent the client from becoming a free rider.

It is fair to say that the derivation procedure whereby Nozick
puts the proprietarian criterion into operation is less impressive
than it first seemed, when it was unclear that agents are assumed
to be moved by moral considerations as well as by rational self-
interest. None the less, it retains a certain persuasive force and it
is unlikely that we shall reject the criterion on the score of operation, at least if we were prepared to endorse it in respect of its
organisation. One further point should be made, however, about
the operation of this standard of justice before we turn to the
third count on which we have to examine it.

There is a distinction between a social charter, in the sense of
a system for resolving political issues, and the allocation of property and power which the charter licenses. One and the same
charter may go with different allocations in so far as different
individuals may occupy positions of economic and legal strength.
As we have characterised it, political assessment has to do with
charters rather than allocations, and criteria of justice, therefore,
need not generally concern themselves with the latter: so long as
they enable us satisfactorily to rank systems of organisation they
need not tell us whether or not to approve of the actual allocation
given under an approved system. However, the point to note
about the proprietarian criterion is that if we use legitimacy as the
test of justice we cannot so easily distinguish the assessment of
charters from the grading of allocations.

The proprietarian is concerned that historical entitlement
should be respected in a society's charter and allocation, not that
a structural pattern should be realised in it. Thus a particular
minimal regime, although its charter is one of which he can

abstractly approve, will not earn his blessing if the allocation of goods within it fails to come of a history of just acquisition and transfer, or of a history in which the effects of any injustice have been rectified. This creates a special problem for the proprietarian since any actual regime will almost certainly uphold an allocation that stems from an unjust and unrectified history. Nozick might approve of an amended US constitution but his focus on history rather than structure would force him to withhold approval from the society, since it is fairly obvious that the holdings of present-day Red Indians are less than they might have been under a non-violent colonisation by Europeans. The problem for the proprietarian is that of framing a principle for rectifying allocations, even allocations under the preferred minimal dispensation. Although it is one which he brings upon himself, this is a pressing difficulty since, as Nozick admits, no one has given more than the bare outline of such a principle.

> The principle of rectification presumably will make use of
> its best estimate of subjunctive information about what
> would have occurred . . . if the injustice had not taken
> place. If the actual description of holdings turns out not to
> be one of the descriptions yielded by the principle, then
> one of the descriptions yielded must be realised. (ASU,
> pp. 152–3)

The third count on which any criterion of justice calls to be examined is in respect of its normative outcome. Even if we are prepared to pass the proprietarian criterion on organisation and operation, we must ask whether the consequences of applying it are sufficiently in line with our judgments about more or less particular matters for us to think that it expresses the demands of justice. Does the criterion generally fit with our intuitive sense of what is politically right and wrong? Even if it forces some changes of mind upon us, does it in most cases endorse what we find unobjectionable, and castigate what we see as intolerable? Unless the answer to this question is affirmative, we cannot take the criterion really seriously: whatever else it is, it will not be to us a standard of social justice.

What we have to consider, in the rough, is whether the minimal state is the dispensation of which we would intuitively approve in the circumstances typical of human life. In such circumstances there is moderate scarcity and a measure of conflict and the question is whether we would find ourselves able to accept as just the resolutions of associated problems to which a minimal charter might give rise. It is notorious that under a *laissez faire* regime inequalities of wealth will quite naturally arise. Differences of fortune and effort will quickly disturb even a perfectly egalitarian distribution and inequalities will compound as the richer, being less and less dependent on exchange, are able to drive ever harder bargains with the poorer. What we have to ask, in particular, is whether we can rejoice in the blessing that the proprietarian criterion would give to such inequalities of distribution.

My own response to this question is that the inequalities are intolerable, particularly in view of the compounding effect, an effect magnified in the succession of generations and the hardening of class divisions. Nozick's slogan, 'From each as they choose, to each as they are chosen' (ASU, p. 160) licenses a system in which the wealthy and their successors can maintain economic and legal privileges indefinitely and in which the less well-off are caught in an endless cycle of relative deprivation. Things might not work out so badly, but then again they might do so, and I should not want to have accepted an account of justice which made it impossible for me to find fault with the result. If anything is unjust, I believe that a regime of inherited privilege and deprivation is so and I cannot have any truck with a criterion of justice that fails to achieve reflective equilibrium with such a central tenet of mine. At this level one is forced back on bedrock intuition and argument looks as much like confession as it does like dialectic: the reader must consider his own intuitive responses and see whether or not he has the stomach to be a proprietarian.

This comment may be slightly premature, however, for what one may try to do in convincing an opponent is to subvert his intuitions by showing that they derive from questionable assumptions or carry unacceptable corollaries. Nozick indeed is ingenious at this activity. Thus he suggests that unequal distribution seems intolerable to many people only because they think of what is distributed as if it were manna from heaven, and not the product of individuals (ASU, p. 198). And again he argues that while we may intuitively recoil from inequality, we are even more opposed intuitively to slavery and this is in perfect parallel to the redistributive regime whereby such inequality might be remedied (ASU, pp. 290–2). How can someone in my position respond to such challenges?

The manna from heaven charge, although it may reveal an uncritical assumption that often bolsters egalitarian attitudes, seems to me to go wide of the mark. What I take to underlie my objection to the cycle of inequality described above is the idea that so far as possible unfair advantage ought to be eliminated in human exchanges, the accumulating advantage envisaged in our scenario being unfair. We shall have more to say later on this notion of fairness when we come to discuss the contractarian approach associated with John Rawls.

Nozick's other charge, that if we embrace the redistributive state we ought also to espouse slavery, is developed in his engaging 'Tale of the Slave' (ASU, pp. 290–2). The tale is about a slave who is badly treated by his master but whose lot is gradually improved. He is treated according to rule, and not at whim; he is rewarded, as are his fellow slaves, on the basis of need or merit or whatever; he is given free time; he is allowed to earn wages and merely has a portion appropriated by his master; he is dealt with according to the wish of his fellow slaves; he is dealt with, not on an individual basis, but according to general policies on which the others agree for the treatment of slaves; he is given a voice, and eventually a vote, in the formation of these policies. Nozick's challenge is to say at what point, if any, the slave ceases to be a slave. The defender of the redistributive regime, assuming that he disapproves of slavery, must draw the line somewhere since the final fate of the slave seems to be very close to that of a subject in such a regime. But where can a line be rationally drawn?

The argument is engaging but, again, it is hardly overwhelming. There are differences, as there are similarities, between the cases described, and someone who believes in the redistributive state is bound to find one or other of these significant. Thus he might say that the important difference between slavery and such a state is that the purposes served by redistribution under the political dispensation are bound, in virtue of the electoral sanction, to be ones that commend themselves to the bulk of people. Anyone who believes in the implementation of certain distributive ideals by government is surely going to find this difference significant enough for drawing the line required. Thus Nozick's challenge, as indeed he foresees (ASU, pp. 277–9), can be easily met.

This marks an end to our ruminations on the merits of the proprietarian criterion. We have raised questions about it under each of our three headings: organisation, operation and output. So far as the first goes we raised complaints about the unanalysability of natural rights, the difficulty of establishing that something is a natural right, and the connection, which is scarcely suppressed by proprietarians, between natural rights and welfare. On the operation of the criterion we drew attention to the switch whereby moral irreproachability is given a motivational role in the derivation of the minimal state, thus weakening the force of the argument, and we commented on the difficulty which the proprietarian must find in meeting his own ideal of assessing allocations as well as charters. Finally we noted that the normative counsel of the proprietarian criterion will be found uncompelling by anyone who recoils from the inequalities associated with *laissez faire* regimes and that the intuitive base of such rejection is not easily dismantled by considerations such as Nozick brings forward.

Bibliographical note

The main reading relevant to this chapter is *Anarchy, State and Utopia*, Blackwell, Oxford, 1974. The appropriate references are given in the text. The initial complaint about natural rights is that the analysis suggested is not a decomposition of the concept, trading in terms from the same family. On the nature of such a decomposition see the editor's introduction to Myles Brand, ed., *The Nature of Causation*, University of Illinois Press, Urbana, 1976. Notice that a criterion which grounds judgments of justice, as distinct merely from generalising them, will have to satisfy the general intuitions mentioned in chapter 4, as well as achieving reflective equilibrium with intuitions on particular matters of justice: all of the criteria considered in this text aspire to a grounding role. The Lockean proviso on acquisition derives from *Two Treatises of Government*, ed. Peter Laslett, Cambridge University Press, 1963. Nozick explicitly opts for one of two possible interpretations, specifying that the position of others must be worsened by their no longer being at liberty to use the thing, and not in any other way, for the proviso to operate. The Lockean theory of acquisition, and other comparable theories, are discussed in Lawrence Becker, *Property Rights*, Routledge & Kegan Paul, London, 1977.

Part IV   The utilitarian criterion of justice

11 Justice as welfare

It appears that legitimacy, in the sense of the satisfaction of natural rights, will not do as a test of justice. The rights invoked in the criterion are dubious metaphysical constructions and, assuming that the criterion may be applied in the manner of Nozick's derivation, the results of respecting them are scarcely in line with the intuitions which most people profess on matters of social justice. But if we reject the path of the proprietarian where should we next turn in our search for a criterion of justice? We may take our cue from history and consider the utilitarian approach which, about the beginning of the nineteenth century, usurped the proprietarianism that had been dominant since Locke. The father of utilitarianism was the English philosopher and reformer Jeremy Bentham and one of the keynotes of his thinking is caught in a famous remark from his essay 'Anarchical Fallacies': 'Natural rights is simple nonsense: natural and imprescriptible rights, rhetorical nonsense – nonsense upon stilts.'

Bentham sought to replace such nonsense with something that was less immaterial and that had greater motivational force. He found what he was looking for in the notion of welfare, and in particular human welfare: this he usually referred to as pleasure or happiness though it also came to be known as utility. He claimed to be inspired to his utilitarianism by the eighteenth-century Scottish thinker, David Hume. In his *Treatise of Human Nature* Hume had diagnosed our disposition to approve or disapprove of something morally, arguing that we were socially conditioned to approve of what was useful to people and society, and to disapprove of what was noxious. Bentham turned this diagnosis into an analysis, proposing that the good was what was useful to mankind – what produced happiness – and the bad was what was otherwise. The analysis had the effect of removing any religious or metaphysical aura that may have attached to the notions of goodness or badness and it opened up the possibility of pursing ethical and political evaluation in an empirical spirit.

The criterion of justice suggested by this analysis was that among a set of rival social charters, or rival resolutions of a particular political issue, that one is best which produces the greatest amount of happiness. In the popular forum a common formulation of this criterion, and it had received the blessing of Bentham, spoke of the greatest happiness of the greatest number. It is worth noting that this expression is a source of ambiguity and is better dropped. Suppose that we have a population of 100 people and that we are considering the relative attractions of two plans A and B. If we scale utility between 0 and 10, we find that the implementation of plan A would put 70 people at level 7 of utility or happiness, 20 at level 5 and 10 at level 1, while the implementation of B would put 50 at level 7 and 50 at level 6. On an assessment of these plans by their tendency to produce happiness B must win, for it gives 650 units of utility against 600 given by A. But if we had claimed to be concerned not just with the greatest happiness, but with the greatest happiness of the greatest number, it is not clear to which plan we would have awarded victory. We might have conferred the laurels on B, thus not attaching any significance to the phrase 'of the greatest number', or we might have selected A as the winner on the grounds that it puts 70 people at level 7 of utility against the 50 that B puts there. But this second line seems not to square with the intentions of the utilitarian, from which it follows that we are well advised to drop the troublesome phrase from the slogan. The goal of political planning is nothing more complex on the utilitarian approach than the maximisation of the happiness of people.

But even this formulation, it should be noted, is often said to be ambiguous in other respects. Happiness may be understood positively as something over and beyond unobstructed consciousness or negatively as something consequent on the removal of interference. In which sense is a utilitarian such as Bentham concerned with its promotion? The answer, most probably, is that Bentham would deny the significance of the distinction and represent happiness as being produced in ever-increasing quantity when pain is gradually removed and pleasure is then induced in its place. A second ambiguity arises from the fact that the greatest happiness may be taken in the sense of greatest aggregate, or greatest average, happiness. The aggregate happiness in a society is got by adding up the utility figure for each of the N people in the population, the average is derived by dividing this total result by N. In response to this ambiguity the utilitarian has reason to deny once again the importance of the distinction. The dispute between an aggregate and average utilitarianism is nothing more than a verbal wrangle except when the number of people who should exist is in question. The main example of where this happens is in the assessment of population policy, an issue in intergenerational justice of the kind that we put aside at the beginning of chapter 2. When one wants to judge the desirability of a drop or a rise in the rate of population expansion it will make a difference to concern oneself with average rather than aggregate happiness, since the size of the population whose happiness is under consideration varies as one considers the different plans.

To return, however, to Bentham, it may be useful to quote at length from his *Introduction to the Principles of Morals and Legislation* in order to give a sense of the empirical approach that he recommended to tasks of evaluation. The following passage gives his famous six-step procedure for assessing the worth of any proposed course of action:

To take an exact account then of the general tendency of any act, by which the interests of a community are affected, proceed as follows. Begin with any one person of those whose interests seem most immediately to be affected by it: and take an account,

1 Of the value of each distinguishable pleasure which appears to be produced by it in the first instance.
2 Of the value of each pain which appears to be produced by it in the first instance.
3 Of the value of each pleasure which appears to be produced by it after the first. This constitutes the fecundity of the first pleasure and the impurity of the first pain.
4 Of the value of each pain which appears to be produced by it after the first. This constitutes the fecundity of the first pain, and the impurity of the first pleasure.
5 Sum up all the values of all the pleasures on the one side, and those of all the pains on the other. The balance, if it be on the side of pleasure, will give the good tendency of the act upon the whole, with respect to the interests of that individual person; if on the side of pain, the bad tendency of it upon the whole.
6 Take an account of the number of persons whose interests appear to be concerned; and repeat the above process with respect to each. Sum up the numbers expressive of the degrees of good tendency, which the act has, with respect to each individual, in regard to

whom the tendency of it is good upon the whole: do this again with respect to each individual, in regard to whom the tendency of it is bad upon the whole. Take the balance; which, if on the side of pleasure, will give the general good tendency of the act, with respect to the total number or community of individuals concerned; if on the side of pain, the general evil tendency, with respect to the same community.

As it is depicted here, and as it remains with most of its later defenders, utilitarianism offers not just a criterion of justice whereby institutional arrangements can be assessed but also a criterion of morality whereby the actions of individuals can be evaluated. It represents a personal philosophy designed to guide one in one's day-to-day behaviour as well as a political philosophy constructed for the purpose of sorting out one's social visions. The feature is worth remarking because it explains why much of the contemporary discussion of utilitarianism belongs to the province of ethics rather than politics. Philosophers concerned with utilitarianism, whether as enemies or enthusiasts, have tended mostly to concentrate on problems such as the following: whether the utilitarian should consider the utility of a particular action in its own right or only the utility of the rule of action instantiated in the particular example; whether it is possible to have a smoothly functioning society in which each individual is a committed ethical utilitarian and is known by others to be such; and whether concerning oneself with always producing the greatest utility possible entails emotional dismantlement, involving neglect of one's intimates, where that is deemed necessary, and even neglect of the self that one conceives oneself to be. Interesting though they are, these questions will be ignored by us, for the reason that they relate to utilitarianism in the ethical rather than the political sense.

As a political doctrine utilitarianism became a dominant force in nineteenth-century England, being invoked in support of various social causes by Bentham and his followers. Its outstanding advocate was John Stuart Mill whose father, James Mill, was a contemporary and associate of Bentham's. John Stuart Mill made utilitarianism the basis for demanding the democratic and related reforms which characterised the Victorian era. The doctrine also achieved an important standing in academic circles in this period, partly because of Mill and partly through the efforts of more retiring scholars, such as the Cambridge philosopher and social theorist, Henry Sidgwick. One of its greatest successes was to become the orthodox measure of progress in the emerging discipline of economics. Welfare economics, the evaluation of the changes which economists seek to chart and control, remained resolutely utilitarian up until the 1930s.

Our exegetical and historical remarks leave us with a criterion of justice that is striking for its simplicity, a feature which has probably accounted for its widespread success. The just social charter is required, not to meet obscure metaphysical constraints such as natural rights represent, but merely to ensure that more happiness is brought about in a population ruled by the charter than would be realised by any alternative. In the remainder of this chapter we shall look in detail at two further aspects of this criterion, the one having to do with its meaning and the other with the method of its proof.

The meaning question arises in connection with the concept of happiness itself. Our criterion remains something less than luminous so long as we fail to clarify exactly what it is that happiness is. For Bentham it was synonymous with pleasure and, while pleasure was not restricted to the satisfaction of distinctively biological desires, it was thought to be like such satisfaction in being a mental state capable of quantitative variation along a number of dimensions: in intensity and duration, for example, purity and fecundity. This conception of happiness, whatever the qualifications to which it was subjected, tended to give pride of place to physical pleasure and so John Stuart Mill was led to assert that utilitarianism concerned itself not just with quantity, but also with quality, of pleasure. The concession was unfortunate, although Mill did not see this, because in making something other than pleasure important, say in putting pleasure of the intellect above pleasure of the palate, it meant a retreat from utilitarianism, strictly understood.

The tradition among utilitarians in this century, especially those concerned with welfare economics, has been to give up Bentham's notion of happiness as a quantitatively variable mental state or sensation. What is put in its place is a conception of happiness as equivalent to the satisfaction of wants or desires. This approach breaks the connection between happiness and sensation and it blocks the sybaritic interpretation which has sometimes been put on the utilitarian goal. It now appears that happiness may mean as many different things as there are different human desires and, just as we should have thought, that one man's happiness may be another man's hell. In what follows I propose that we should adopt this reading of what it is that the utilitarian seeks to have maximised. Want-satisfaction has problems of its own as a goal of social planning, and we shall see some of these in a moment, but it is not such a contentious psychological construct as the pleasure which Bentham had in mind. There may not be any single state answering to Bentham's specifications but there certainly is such a thing as the satisfaction of human desires. The move from pleasure to want-satisfaction allows us to describe utilitarianism as concerned with welfare, for on at least one conception of people's welfare it consists in their having their aspirations fulfilled. This term is more appealing than 'happiness' or 'utility' in the presentation of utilitarianism, since it does not have the old psychologistic associations. Hence the preference for it in the title of this chapter.

Even when happiness has been equated with the satisfaction of desires, there remain questions about exactly what it means. The utilitarian must decide for example if such satisfaction includes getting rid of a desire by persuasion, deception or illusion as well as fulfilling it in the literal sense of bringing about the state of affairs that is found attractive. In this case I suggest that only a slide back towards the psychologistic notion of happiness could justify the construal of satisfaction as consisting in the cessation of desire, however that is attained, rather than in its literal fulfilment. Other problems, however, do not lend themselves to such ready resolution. In particular, and this is the only source of problems that will be mentioned here, the utilitarian will have great difficulty in deciding what limit to put on the wants with which a social planner should be concerned; as we shall see, some limit is certainly required, but it is far from clear which is appropriate.

What makes it certain that a limit must be put on the wants to which the utilitarian planner pays attention is that some of the wants that people have presuppose the acceptance of a non-utilitarian conception of justice. As a proprietarian Mr Smith will want to have a minimal state established but it can be no part of the utilitarian's ambition to try to ensure the satisfaction of that desire, unless it happens that the minimal state is the regime that will bring about the greatest satisfaction of the other sorts of wants that people have in that society. Were utilitarianism to give heed to such political desires it would tend to go over into majoritarianism, suggesting that the important thing in politics is that people get the social order they want, rather than the order which satisfies their wants.

So much for the clear-cut case. The difficult cases, and I will not try to adjudicate on them here, can be illustrated by the two examples of ethically based desires and other-regarding desires. Among the wants that individuals have are some that stem from the espousal of a non-utilitarian personal or ethical philosophy. Our Mr Smith may be a rigorous puritan, for example, who wants to have little truck with earthly satisfactions. Should the utilitarian planner try to take account of such a want or should he argue that the man does not know what is good for him, being misled by an ill-conceived ethic, and so discount this puritanical aspiration in his calculations? The issue is not one that allows of easy judgment. At first the temptation is to say that ethically based desires should indeed be discounted in utilitarian planning but further reflection raises doubts, for one may well baulk at the number of wants that this restriction would rule out and one may wonder at the utilitarian's authority for imposing it: after all his utilitarianism concerns political matters only and it is unclear how he is able to judge on the merits or demerits of personal philosophies.

People's desires are sometimes distinguished into the self-regarding ones that they hold in respect of themselves and the other-regarding desires that they entertain on behalf of their fellows. Thus apart from the things which he wants for himself, Mr Smith may wish all sorts of good and bad things on other members of his society, whether by name or by group denomination. Ought the utilitarian planner to be concerned with these desires of people *vis-à-vis* others as well as with their desires in their own regard? It may well seem not, especially since such desires include the yearning of the bigot for the humiliation of those he despises. But then again, perhaps such a yearning can be put down as a want that stems from the acceptance of a very distorted non-utilitarian criterion of justice. There are some other-regarding desires, such as those that the parent has in respect of his children, which it seems arbitrary to discount in utilitarian planning, and to put all such wants beyond the reach of political consideration might be to do more harm than good. Once again though we shall leave the issue open.

We promised some remarks not just on the meaning of the utilitarian criterion but on the method of its proof. In the chapter after next we shall examine the case to be made for utilitarianism on the grounds of reflective equilibrium with our intuitive judgments on particular issues of justice. The question of proof arises here because some philosophers have suggested that a case can be made for utilitarianism on independent grounds. Sidgwick, for example, thought that it was supported by a direct intuition as to the value of happiness and more recently Ronald Dworkin has urged that the doctrine can hope to be grounded only in the intuition that people have the right to be treated as equals: he says that the only reason why it might make sense to prefer a system giving greater aggregate happiness to one giving less is that, considering the wants of each person equally, we find that the system gives people more of what they want overall, even though some individuals may fare less well under it. In the remaining portion of this chapter I wish to consider a more famous argument than either of these for the truth of utilitarianism. It appears in John Stuart Mill's classic piece *Utilitarianism*, a work in which the author agrees elsewhere with Bentham that the utilitarian criterion is not susceptible of proof in any strict sense of the term. The deduction of the criterion, whatever weight Mill thought it had, is a notoriously fallacious piece of reasoning, but it will be salutary to examine its weaknesses.

Mill's proof is summarised in a single paragraph and it is worth quoting this in full:

> The only proof capable of being given that an object is visible is that people actually see it. The only proof that a sound is audible is that people hear it: and so of the other sources of our experience. In like manner, I apprehend, (1) *the sole evidence it is possible to produce that anything is desirable, is that people do actually desire it*. If the end which the utilitarian doctrine proposes to itself were not, in theory and practice, acknowledged to be an end, nothing could ever convince any person that it was so. No reason can be given why the general happiness is desirable, except that (2) *each person, so far as he believes it to be attainable, desires his own happiness*. This, however, being a fact, we have not only all the proof which the case admits of, but all which it is possible to require, that happiness is good: that (3) *each person's happiness is a good to that person*, and (4) *the general happiness, therefore, a good to the aggregate of all persons*. Happiness has made out its title as *one* of the ends of conduct, and consequently one of the criteria of morality. (*Utilitarianism* Chapter 4)

(In later paragraphs Mill argues that it is the only end, and the sole criterion, to the extent that things other than happiness are desired only as a part of it or a means to it.)

In this paragraph the conclusion that the general happiness is a good to the aggregate of all persons – which modulates into the utilitarian criterion after the manner indicated in my parenthesis – is derived from the three clauses which, like the conclusion itself, I have put in italics and numbered. It is clear that 3 is supposed to follow from 1 and 2 and that 4, the conclusion, is meant to derive from 3. Let us now examine the components and the composition of the argument.

Premise 1, the proposition that something is proved to be desirable by being desired, is meant to follow from the considerations on visibility and audibility which are mentioned in the opening sentences. It does not follow from them, however, and, moreover, it is false. As was long ago pointed out, where 'visible' means 'can be seen' and 'audible' 'can be heard', 'desirable' has a prescriptive connotation, meaning 'ought to be desired'. And while the fact that something is so proves that it can be so – *ab esse ad posse valet illatio*, the scholastics used to say – it goes no way towards proving that it ought to be so. Thus, that something is desired does not prove that it is desirable. Indeed, and this shows the falsity of the proposition, many things which we are ready enough to acknowledge that we desire are scarcely such that we would proclaim them to be desirable.

Since proposition 1 is false the third proposition, which is meant to be derived from propositions 1 and 2, is certainly unproven. Before we ask whether it is also false, we may pause for a moment over proposition 2, according to which each person desires his own happiness, so far as he thinks that he can attain it. This looks like a statement of psychological hedonism, asserting that it is an empirically ascertainable if often overlooked fact, that people concern themselves only with the payoffs to themselves which their actions are likely to give. This need not be taken to suggest, as opponents have often wanted to argue, that people focus only on the psychological states which will be induced in them by their actions and the outcomes of their actions. But it remains still a highly unfetching proposition. More important than this, what must also be said is that if Mill means to put forward psychological hedonism in his second proposition, then it is arguable that he is making a move which undermines utilitarianism. For if it is held that as a matter of psychological fact people are incorrigible egoists, how can it be hoped that in their political planning, and even in their personal lives – Mill is also an ethical utilitarian – they will concern themselves with producing the greatest aggregate happiness? The fact that psychological hedonism is controversial, and even more, the fact that it runs counter to the intentions of utilitarianism, suggests that we ought to exercise charity and interpret Mill's proposition 2 in some other way. Our earlier comments on happiness suggest that we should take it merely to say that each person desires his own want-satisfaction and, while it must remain a mystery how Mill ever thought that anything could follow from such tautology, this interpretation has the merit of making the claim come out as true.

But let us now take up proposition 3 and ask whether it is true or false, granted that it is certainly not proven. 'Each person's happiness is a good to that person': that is, each person ought to desire his own happiness. Here the same ambiguity in the word 'happiness' comes up as in the second proposition, but unless we

115

are prepared to revise our earlier remarks we must now take the term to mean 'want-satisfaction'. Interpreting on these lines, we take Mill to be saying that each man ought to desire that his actual desires be satisfied. And, except for someone of a bizarre moral standpoint, that must seem to be a grossly mistaken view. We have little option but to conclude that the proposition is false.

Finally then to the conclusion of the argument. Since proposition 3 is false, the alleged fact that proposition 4 follows from it does nothing to establish proposition 4. And this failure is compounded, for only a little examination reveals that in any case 4 does not follow from 3. That each person ought to desire his own happiness does not prove that each person ought to desire everybody's happiness any more than that each person ought to mind his own business proves that each person ought to mind everybody's business. We are left then with the question whether the fourth proposition, unproven though it is, is a statement that we wish to accept. And this resolves into the object of our inquiry in the next two chapters: to decide whether the utilitarian principle is something around which we can reconstruct our political intuitions.

In this chapter we have been introduced to the second of the three conceptions of justice considered in this text. We began with an account of Bentham's original thought that the justice of a social charter could be measured by the contribution of the charter to human happiness. We discussed some ambiguities in Bentham's formulation of his utilitarian criterion and we remarked on the influence of the criterion among nineteenth-century thinkers such as John Stuart Mill and Henry Sidgwick. The point was made that utilitarianism is as much a personal philosophy as a political one and that most contemporary discussion of utilitarian questions relates to its ethical face. We examined some problems with the meaning of happiness, opting to construe it as want-satisfaction, and agreeing that some limit needed to be put on the wants which the utilitarian is supposed to take into account. Finally we drew attention to attempts to vindicate utilitarianism by direct intuition or proof and we analysed in detail Mill's infamous argument in his essay *Utilitarianism*.

Bibliographical note

The classic sources of utilitarianism are Jeremy Bentham, *An Introduction to the Principles of Morals and Legislation* (1789), Hafner, New York, 1970, J. S. Mill, *Utilitarianism* (1863), Dent, London, 1972, and Henry Sidgwick, *The Methods of Ethics* (1874), Macmillan, London 1962. For a useful short history see John

Plamenatz, *The English Utilitarians*, rev. edn, Blackwell, Oxford, 1958. The distinctions between negative and positive, average and aggregate, utilitarianism are drawn by Smart in J. J. C. Smart and Bernard Williams, *Utilitarianism: For and Against*, Cambridge University Press, 1973. This book also contains discussion of, and gives further references on, the issues mentioned in connection with ethical utilitarianism. Another useful account of such questions, with a strong historical slant, is Anthony Quinton, *Utilitarian Ethics*, Macmillan, London, 1973. That utilitarianism is concerned with the quality of happiness or pleasure, as well as with its quantity, is maintained by J. S. Mill in *Utilitarianism*. The construal of happiness as want-satisfaction is discussed in Brian Barry, *Political Argument*, Routledge & Kegan Paul, London, 1965, chapter 3. Problems with how to limit the wants considered by the utilitarian are discussed in Ronald Dworkin, *Taking Rights Seriously*, Duckworth, London, 1978, chapters 9 and 12, and in Jonathan Glover, *Causing Death and Saving Lives*, Penguin, Harmondsworth, 1975, chapter 4. Sidgwick's proposal about the grounding of utilitarianism is made in his *Methods of Ethics* and Dworkin's in *Taking Rights Seriously*. For commentaries on Mill's deduction, with references to earlier criticisms, see Quinton, *Utilitarian Ethics* and Alan Ryan, *John Stuart Mill*, Routledge & Kegan Paul, London, 1974.

12   The directives of welfare

In parallel to our treatment of proprietarianism the question which we now have to ask about the utilitarian criterion is: what charter does this conception of justice recommend for the organisation of social life? To be a proprietarian is to espouse the minimal state, at least if one is persuaded by Nozick's argument that this regime would rationally and morally emerge in a situation such as Locke's state of nature. What dispensation commands the affections of the utilitarian; or does his criterion of justice leave him without defined preferences over the alternative charters imaginable?

Since the utilitarian says that the just charter for any society is that which produces the greatest happiness among its members, he is naturally embarrassed by the question posed. His criterion of justice means that he cannot say which arrangement is desirable for a given society until he knows something about the wants of the members and the degrees to which these wants are satisfied by the different charters available. There is no single charter which can be guaranteed always and everywhere to produce the greatest happiness and therefore there is no answer to the abstract question of which charter is the one preferred. As a political philosophy utilitarianism does not entail a substantive policy in the fashion of its proprietarian or indeed contractarian counterpart. In place of a material policy it offers a method for policy-making. The utilitarian is not allowed to attach himself to a particular dispensation, cherishing it as the unique solution to the political issues that human beings encounter, but he is enabled to discover which of the dispensations in the offing is the just one to institute in a given society. All that he has to find out is which arrangement best satisfies the wants of the individuals in that community.

What I propose to do in this chapter, in view of the fact that utilitarianism has no prescription to offer in the abstract for the organisation of social life, is to examine the possibility of implementing the method of policy-making which it puts forward in place of such a prescription. From its earliest days the critics of utilitarianism have argued that the doctrine is founded in a myth, since we can never know what will produce the greatest pleasure or want-satisfaction, not being able to see into the minds of human beings. The point of the chapter is to see whether this criticism can be rebutted; unless a rebuttal is available there is nothing further to say about utilitarianism, for a political philosophy which fails to express any determinate demands can hardly claim to formulate the requirements of justice. Taking happiness in the sense of want-satisfaction, what I shall try to show is that there is a sense in which the utilitarian may claim to be able to measure it, establishing that one charter or policy satisfies people's wants more fully than any alternatives. I will characterise a method-ological procedure to which the utilitarian might help himself. The procedure is not one that is characterised in the literature although it is built on notions familiar from the writings of economists and philosophers on decision theory. It should be mentioned that these notions are simplified in the presentation and that a number of important qualifications and refinements are omitted: this is surely excusable in a text such as ours, especially in view of the fact that readers unacquainted with decision theory may well find even our uncomplicated presentation difficult to follow.

There are two outstanding problems in the way of measuring want-satisfaction and they respectively concern the calibration of an individual's degrees of satisfaction, say in the prospects offered by rival political dispensations, and the comparison of such degrees of satisfaction across individuals. Instead of degrees of satisfaction it is more usual nowadays to speak of intensities of preference for reasons that will later become obvious. The cali-bration problem is that of establishing, not just that an individual prefers A to B, B to C, and C to D, but that he prefers A to B more intensely than B to C, B to C more intensely than C to D, and so on through other four-term comparisons. In parallel the comparison problem is that of saying for example whether one person's preference for A over B is more or less intense than another's for B over A.

The calibration problem is important because if we are to measure the relative effects of different destinies on the want-satisfaction of an individual we need to have more than ordinal information on his preferences among the destinies. If a given destiny features A rather than the less preferred B offered by an alternative, but if it also means the realisation of D in place of the more preferred C, we cannot estimate whether it gives more satisfaction than the alternative until we know whether the indi-

119

vidual prefers *A* to *B* more intensely than he does *C* to *D*. The further information required is of a cardinal variety. The scale on which it is represented will fix, not just the order of the person's preferences, but also the interval between preferences. If it is displayed in a vertical line, with the most preferred alternative at the top and the least at the bottom, then it will enable us to read off relative intensities of preference by the intervals which it leaves between the intermediate points. If *A* is preferred to *B* more than *B* to *C*, and *B* to *C* more than *C* to *D*, then the line might look for example as in Figure 1.

A

B

C

D

Figure 1

It may be mentioned in passing here, although the point is too technical to concern us seriously, that while any cardinal scale is required to fix interval, giving answers to questions of four-term comparison, the ideal scale also fixes unit and origin. Unit is fixed when the ratio between intervals is mathematically determinate, origin when there is a uniquely correct mathematical representation for the starting point of the scale. The system for measuring length in middle sized objects by inches, feet and yards gives us zero as origin and it also fixes unit, for it enables us to put a mathematically determinate construction on the ratios between intervals: we do not just know that the interval between the lengths of a given pair of objects is larger than the interval between another pair; we can also determine that the first interval is one and a half times as large as the second, or whatever. It would be marvellous if we had such a cardinal scale for measuring intensities of preference but our purposes would be satisfactorily served by a scale which, although it left unit and origin arbitrary, established limits sufficient to fix the comparison of intervals. Such a scale would be adequately expressed in any assignment of numbers to the items ranked, which had the property of preserving interval comparison. Our *D* to *A* might be given the numbers 1, 2, 4, 8, or 2, 4, 8, 16, or indeed 9, 13, 21, 37, for each of these sequences gives the same answers to questions of the form: is the interval between A and B greater than the interval between B and C? (It can be shown that if a given sequence is transformed through the multiplication of each member by a positive number and the addition to it of any number, positive or negative, the resulting sequence will preserve the same ranking of intervals as the original: the scale, as is sometimes said, is unique up to a positive linear transformation.)

The comparison problem is equally important with the calibration one, for it will be no good if we know of a given political scheme the utility that it has for each individual *vis-à-vis* alternatives, but cannot compare these utilities, the one with the other. Suppose that there are two rival schemes S' and S''. In order to know which produces the greater want-satisfaction, even for a population of two people, we have to be able to align the degrees of satisfaction that they produce in each person. Thus one individual might prefer S', the other S'', and if we are to make a utilitarian judgment either way we will have to know in whom the greater degree of satisfaction is produced by his getting his way: or equivalently, in whom the preference for his chosen scheme over the alternative is the more intense.

Many economists became persuaded in the 1930s that the calibration and comparison problems were insoluble and they allowed themselves to be pushed out of their traditional utilitarianism; this led to the development of the 'new welfare economics', a much criticised approach which gave especial importance to the Pareto criterion discussed in chapter 14 below. In retrospect their reaction can be judged to have been over-hasty for already in the 1920s the Cambridge mathematician-cum-philosopher Frank Ramsey had elaborated a method for measuring want-satisfaction on a cardinal scale, a method closely related to one which was independently discovered twenty years later by the founders of game theory, John Von Neumann and Otto Morgenstern. In what follows I provide a rough introduction to the Ramsey method of calibrating preferences, I show how it may be adapted to allow the comparison of intensities of preference across individuals and I characterise a procedure for pressing the method into the service of utilitarianism.

The starting point of the Ramsey method is the so-called *expected utility hypothesis* according to which the value of a gamble (x, y), where x and y are the possible outcomes, is equal to the sum of the values of the outcomes, each of these values being weighted by the probability attaching to the corresponding event. If the gamble is a fair one, and there is an equal chance of either outcome, then the hypothesis has it that the utility of the gamble, $U(g)$, is equal to half the utility of x plus half the utility of y, $\frac{1}{2}U(x) + \frac{1}{2}U(y)$. This hypothesis seems to be a reasonable conjecture although it should be noticed that it assumes an indifference in the subject to taking a risk such as the gamble represents. Were one unduly averse to risk, or unduly attracted to it, the utility of the gamble might come out as correspondingly less than, or greater than, the figure given by $\frac{1}{2}U(x) + \frac{1}{2}U(y)$. Or, to put this in another way, while $U(g)$ might be equal to half the utility of x-after-a-gamble plus half the utility of y-after-a-gamble, i.e. $\frac{1}{2}U(x/g) + \frac{1}{2}U(y/g)$, this latter figure might not coincide with $\frac{1}{2}U(x) + \frac{1}{2}U(y)$.

Putting aside this possibility, and ignoring various related complications, let us assume the truth of the expected utility hypothesis in the sense given. The importance of the hypothesis is that it enables us to calibrate intensities of preference. If someone prefers A over B with the same intensity as he prefers B over C, then $U(A) - U(B) = U(B) - U(C)$ and $U(B) = \frac{1}{2}U(A) + \frac{1}{2}U(C)$, in which case the hypothesis tells us that the person is indifferent between having B for certain and being given a fair gamble that may produce A or C. Thus if we discover such indifference we may take this as evidence that the interval on the person's preference scale between A and B is the same as the interval between B and C. By a similar line of reasoning, if he prefers A to B more than he prefers B to C, then $U(A) - U(B) > U(B) - U(C)$ and $U(B) < \frac{1}{2}U(A) + \frac{1}{2}U(C)$, in which case the hypothesis entails that the person prefers being given a fair gamble between A and C to having B for certain. It follows then that if we find such a preference on someone's part we may reasonably conclude that the interval on his preference scale between A and B is greater than that between B and C. These two pieces of deduction illustrate how information about someone's dispositions not just to rank his options, but to rank gambles involving them, can reveal his intensities of preference in respect of the options: this, on the assumption that the person chooses in accordance with the expected utility hypothesis. The dispositions in question are sometimes called a person's extended preferences over the options: extended, ordinal preferences give us non-extended, cardinal ones.

Ramsey's method for calibrating preferences exploits this possibility. Suppose we wish to establish the intensities of someone's preferences over certain foods: say, chicken, beef, lamb and pork. The agent prefers chicken to beef, beef to lamb, and lamb to pork, and we want to know how relatively intense these preferences are. The proposed procedure would have us go through the following steps. First, we ascertain the agent's preference ordering and establish chicken and pork respectively at the top and bottom of our scale. Second, we find some event, such as a coin coming up heads, about which he feels neutral and to which he attaches a subjective probability of a half. The event will be neutral if the person's preferences remain the same whether or not he believes it to have taken place. It will have a subjective probability of a half if he is indifferent between the two gambles (heads chicken, tails pork) and (heads pork, tails chicken): this is a consequence of the expected utility hypothesis. Third, we determine the mid-point of the scale as the gamble (heads chicken, tails pork) and we look for a food such that the agent is indifferent between having it for certain and being given that gamble. This food will then be something satisfying the condition that he prefers chicken to it with just the intensity that he prefers it to pork. We could proceed without positive identification but let us suppose that the food is ham. Our fourth step is then to determine the quarter points on the scale as the gambles (heads chicken, tails ham) and (heads ham, tails pork) and to look for foods such that again the agent is indifferent to having them for certain and being given the appropriate gambles. We continue this exploration of extended preferences, establishing more and more points on the scale, until the troublesome beef and lamb are allocated places.

The procedure just described can be illustrated nicely in Figure 2, in which the top and bottom points are arbitrarily given the numbers 1 and 0.

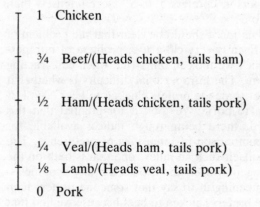

1	Chicken	
¾	Beef/(Heads chicken, tails ham)	
½	Ham/(Heads chicken, tails pork)	
¼	Veal/(Heads ham, tails pork)	
⅛	Lamb/(Heads veal, tails pork)	
0	Pork	

Figure 2

Such a table gives us cardinal information on intensities of preference although it does so without fixing origin or unit. We can rely on it as a source of information on intervals: that is, as a guide to whether the intensity with which one item is preferred to another is the same as, or is greater or less than, the intensity of preference in respect of another pair. However we cannot take the figures seriously in any further regard, for it can be shown that this information is preserved in any sequence of numbers that is a positive linear transformation of the set given.

So much then for the Ramsey method of calibrating preferences. The procedure enables us to solve the cardinality problem encountered by utilitarians and the next stage in our discussion must be to see whether we can also see our way past the parallel problem of comparability. In its original form this is the difficulty of whether it makes sense to say that someone enjoys the same want-satisfaction as another in a particular outcome, or a satisfaction that is greater or less than it by some comparative measure: say, as much greater than it as a third party's is lesser. Recast in terms of intensity of preference, the problem is whether we can meaningfully say that one person prefers one option to another as intensely as, or more or less intensely than, someone else makes a preference in respect of the same or a different pair. An example of the original difficulty is whether we can say that the increase in satisfaction given to person i by the solution of some political issue in fashion S' rather than S'' is greater than the decrease in satisfaction given to person j by the same piece of social organisation. In its recast form, this is the problem of whether we can sensibly report that person i prefers S' to S'' more intensely than person j prefers S'' to S'.

In its revised formulation it should be clear that the problem of interpersonal comparison is very close to a problem of intrapersonal comparison which we took in our stride when constructing the Ramsey procedure. The intrapersonal difficulty is whether it is coherent to say that someone prefers chicken to beef, say, less than he prefers ham to pork. We took it for granted that this could be surmounted, there being rough indices available for establishing such a comparison of intensities of preference. The Ramsey procedure is itself such an index: one that is built on the assumption that the agent follows the expected utility hypothesis. We think that it is meaningful to say that someone prefers ham to pork more than he prefers chicken to beef because we find that he resists being given pork in place of ham more than he resists having chicken replaced by beef; or, to use the Ramsey index, because he prefers a fair gamble between ham and beef to a fair gamble between chicken and pork: $\frac{1}{2}\,U(\text{ham}) + \frac{1}{2}U(\text{beef}) >$

$\frac{1}{2}U$(chicken) + $\frac{1}{2}U$(pork), which means that U(ham) – U(pork) > U(chicken) – U(beef).

If we are prepared to assume that the intrapersonal problem is soluble, it appears only reasonable that we should be just as liberal in respect of the interpersonal one. For here, as in the other case, there are lots of indices whereby we make rough and ready judgments of comparison. On the basis of greater need or greater effort for example I am willing to say that a companion's preference for playing squash over joining me in a trip to the cinema is more intense than my reverse preference. Indeed we even go so far as to judge on the relative intensities of preferences over different pairs. Thus, in dealing with children, we are quite liable to decide that John prefers reading to radio more than Mary prefers sound to silence and that, just as the greater happiness is secured by my playing squash with my companion rather than by my forcing him into going to the cinema, so a greater net balance of satisfaction is achieved among the children if the radio apparatus is turned off.

This line of thinking should give us the courage to surmount the difficulty of interpersonal comparison as boldly as we did its intrapersonal counterpart. It suggests that if we have extended preferences and therefore Ramsey scales or utility functions for two individuals in respect of a set of options then we may reasonably draw comparative corollaries, so long as the scales are mathematically expressed in figures sufficiently aligned to ensure the truth of the comparisons that we can make on an intuitive basis. Thus if we use a scale U_i for person i and a scale U_j for person j, and if we judge intuitively that i prefers S' to S'' more than j prefers S'' to S', then the scales should be given numbers which guarantee that $U_i(S') - U_i(S'')$ is greater than $U_j(S'') - U_j(S')$. This would mean for example that in most circumstances it would not do to make U_i a scale from 0 to 1 and U_j a scale from 100 to 1000.

Let us take our courage in our hands then and begin to construct a strategy for the utilitarian assessment of competing social charters. We may stick to concrete issues and consider how to go about measuring the relative degrees of want-satisfaction produced by the different alternatives in sets of rival policies such as the following: no divorce, circumscribed divorce, divorce at will; market determination of wages and salaries, statutory incomes control, collective bargaining; electoral representation on a proportional basis, electoral representation on the basis of a non-transferable vote; and so on. In every such case we will want to have a Ramsey scale or utility function for each individual over the options involved, and we will want to select that option which a comparison of those scales indicates as the one most likely to produce the highest net balance of satisfaction. But how will we know what slack to leave in the mathematical expression of the different scales: we can hardly be expected to have made intuitive judgments on the relative intensities of preference across the various individuals in the society? Here we may take our cue from an oft quoted remark of Bentham's: each to count for one, and none for more than one. The reasonable line would seem to be that we scale the preferences of the individuals within the same mathematical limits, say between 0 and 1. We cannot hope to determine that one or another individual has a particularly passionate disposition, deserving of a scale with a larger mathematical spread, and in ignorance of such variation we may well treat all as equal.

Unfortunately we are not yet out of the woods. The problem is that if we apply the Ramsey method straightforwardly in seeking someone's relative intensities of preference over a set of political options we shall pick up his political desires rather than his nonpolitical ones: we shall discover which policy he wants, and how strongly he wants it, but we shall still be in ignorance as to which policy is liable best to satisfy his wants. Thus if we present a person with the divorce options, the straightforward procedure will unearth his political preferences on the divorce issue; it will not give us any idea of the relative satisfaction accruing to the individual under the different marital dispensations.

This is an additional problem to those of calibration and comparison, but it can be overcome in a manner that has independent plausibility and should not seem *ad hoc*. Instead of presenting an agent with the divorce options for scaling, we might reasonably put before him as alternatives the various positions under the different options that he is liable to occupy: say, if he is a young unmarried man, such positions as being the son of divorced parents, the unhappy spouse of an undivorceable wife, the unwilling partner in a divorce case, the divorced guardian of his children, and so on through a great range of possibilities. If we had an individual's utilities for such positions we could help ourselves once again to the expected utility hypothesis in order to determine his utility for each of the original options. Each such option can be seen as a gamble between the destinies possible for the person in question and its expected utility will then be the sum of the utilities of the destinies, each such utility being weighted by the probability of the corresponding destiny coming about. Suppose there are five outcomes possible for the individual, a, b, c, d and e, and suppose further that the respective probabilities of their coming about in the event of the option being realised are: $\frac{1}{4}$, $\frac{1}{3}$, $\frac{1}{4}$, $\frac{1}{12}$, $\frac{1}{12}$. In this case the expected utility of the option for the individual will be $\frac{1}{4}U(a) + \frac{1}{3}U(b) + \frac{1}{4}U(c) + \frac{1}{12}U(d) +$

$^1/_{12}U(e)$. The expected utility figure yielded by such a procedure will not reflect the person's political attitude *vis-à-vis* the option, unless he cheats in giving his utilities over the different positions. It may be plausibly taken to represent the prospective want-satisfaction which the dispensation in question holds out for the individual, and to give us just the index we need for a utilitarian assessment.

With this point clarified then we are in a position to describe a procedure for the utilitarian assessment of the competing solutions to any political issue. The procedure can be broken down into five steps.

1 Identify the positions that each individual is liable to occupy under each alternative and link with each such position a probability index of the chance of the individual finding himself within it in the event of the corresponding alternative being selected.

2 Using common mathematical limits, establish for each individual a Ramsey scale or utility function over all the positions that it is possible for him to occupy: this will give the utility of each position for the individual.

3 Compute the expected utility for each person of each alternative by adding together the utilities that he attaches to the positions available to him under that alternative, each of these utilities being weighted by the probability index associated with the corresponding position under 1.

4 Compute the social utility of each alternative by aggregating the figures representing its expected utility for each individual.

5 Select as the just solution to the political issue in question that alternative with the highest social utility.

This procedure for applying the utilitarian criterion of justice will not be universally regarded as convincing. There are all sorts of difficulties that come up with implementing it, not the least of which is that people are required to exercise considerable insight and imagination in placing the prospects of different positions on a Ramsey scale: they have to be able to make a highly sophisticated ranking of those prospects both in relation to one another and in relation to certain gambles. Despite such difficulties however, the procedure is more convincing than the usual proposal for applying the utilitarian criterion. This proposal is that the utilitarian assessor of political schemes should adopt the stance of impartial spectator on the individuals in a society and, after identifying with each of these individuals in order to get a grasp on their different interests, should make a decision on their behalf as to which scheme will best satisfy their wants. A utilitarian who could invoke the outcome of our procedure in defence of a given scheme would earn a hearing more readily than one who could only claim the mantle of the impartial spectator in arguing that the scheme promised the greatest net balance of satisfaction. The procedure offers a better guarantee of objectivity than the less formal strategy.

In this chapter we saw that utilitarianism may recommend different charters for different societies, depending on the desires of the individuals involved. We decided to investigate the possibility of applying the criterion convincingly and in particular the prospect of overcoming the problems of calibrating and comparing degrees of want satisfaction. We outlined the Ramsey method for measuring intensities of preference as a solution to the first problem and we argued that the second problem could be solved on parallel lines. Finally we suggested a procedure for adapting that method to the service of utilitarian assessment, solving along the way a third problem raised by the interference of political aspirations with the desires whose satisfaction interests the utilitarian.

Bibliographical note

The calibration and comparison of utilities are discussed, with characteristic clarity and verve, in Chapter 7 and 7* of Amartya Sen, *Collective Choice and Social Welfare*, Oliver & Boyd, London, 1970. Sen's treatment deals more with the Von Neumann and Morgenstern approach to calibration than it does with Ramsey's. Ramsey's method is presented in 'Truth and Probability' in the recent collection of his writings, *Foundations*, ed. D. H. Mellor, Routledge & Kegan Paul, London, 1978. For a beautiful presentation of Ramsey's ideas see Richard Jeffrey, *The Logic of Decision*, McGraw-Hill, New York, 1965, chapter 3. The approach taken above to the problem of interpersonal comparison is heavily indebted to an article of Jeffrey's, 'On Interpersonal Utility Theory', *Journal of Philosophy*, vol. 68, 1971. For argument in defence of such comparison see Ilmar Waldner, 'The Empirical Meaningfulness of Interpersonal Utility Comparisons', *Journal of Philosophy*, vol. 69, 1972. The impartial spectator approach to utilitarian assessment is discussed in John Rawls, *A Theory of Justice*, Oxford University Press, 1972, pp. 183–92. One of its staunchest defenders is R. M. Hare; see for example his *Freedom and Reason*, Oxford University Press, 1963.

13   Welfare under scrutiny

The three headings under which we examined the proprietarian criterion of justice were: internal organisation, mode of operation, and normative output. The utilitarian standard calls for scrutiny under the same titles but it happens that we have already pressed its examination under the first two. Its internal organisation comes into question mainly because of the obscurity attaching to the concept of happiness and this issue we discussed and resolved in chapter 11: the resolution consisted of construing happiness as want-satisfaction, in particular the satisfaction of wants other than those which presuppose the acceptance of a non-utilitarian political philosophy; we acknowledged that further limits might be required on the wants considered but we left that matter open. The operation of the utilitarian criterion of justice is in question in so far as it is unclear how the measure can be applied in identifying the just social charter or the just solution to some political issue and this question we settled more or less satisfactorily in the chapter just completed: we outlined a procedure for determining which of a set of rival political schemes is likely to produce the highest net balance of satisfaction in a community, a procedure that is not described in the literature but which would seem to meet most of the demands that can reasonably be made on the utilitarian.

It remains then, in this chapter, to concern ourselves with the normative output of utilitarianism. The matter which we have to resolve is whether welfare as a definition of justice matches in its consequences the considered judgments that we maintain on particular political issues: whether in this sense the implications of the criterion are in line with our intuitions. The test to which we have to submit utilitarianism is, in John Rawls's phrase, the test of reflective equilibrium. We have to see whether the assessments to which the philosophy would naturally lead are in equilibrium with the judgments over which we are intuitively disposed to stand: this, after we have made all the helpful amendments to our intuitions, which it seems possible to contemplate. Unless we find such a reflective equilibrium between the utilitarian analysis of justice and our intuitive sense of the subject we can have no ground for taking the analysis seriously; it will appear that what we make of justice is something other than what is made of it by the theory and in that case we have no option but to reject the theory.

Are our intuitions, then, the stuff of which utilitarianism is made? We might pursue this question by going through the likely consequences of applying the criterion to the different sorts of issues distinguished in chapter 2, considering in each case whether or not the consequences coincide with our intuitive responses. That, however, would be an exceedingly laborious course to follow and instead I propose to adopt an approach parallel to that which we took in discussing the corresponding question with proprietarianism. In that other case we ignored most of the implications of the proprietarian criterion and went straight to what promised to be the most troubling result: the endorsement which the criterion would give to certain regimes of inherited privilege and deprivation. With utilitarianism it happens that there is also a particular consequence which is widely found to be objectionable and we may turn directly to this in examining the claim of the philosophy to represent, if also partially to reconstruct, our intuitions on particular questions of justice.

The best illustration of the consequence can be given by reference to a small scale issue of distribution. Suppose that we want to decide how best to distribute a bag of sweets among a dozen children. On scheme 1, we might divide the bag equally, giving each child, say, one sweet. On scheme 2, we give the entire bag to the three oldest children and ignore the claims of the others. Which scheme should we adopt, assuming that these are the only alternatives? The embarrassment with the utilitarian criterion is that under a particular, not implausible, circumstance it would have us recommend the unequal allocation. The circumstance is of course that such a distribution produces more aggregate happiness than the alternative. It is not implausible, for the reason that whereas on the first scheme each child is very little pleased, being more tantalised than really fulfilled, on the second the three oldest are satisfied in splendid measure, not just through being given four sweets each but also through having the status of their seniority publicly acknowledged. In such a case it is quite likely that more want-satisfaction is produced in aggregate by the unequal allocation than would have been brought about by giving one sweet to each child.

If we assume that the children have the same titles to the sweets, say because of a promise to the group or because of some service done by them, then it is difficult to conceive of our happily endorsing the inegalitarian distribution. The question of whether we have the stomach for utilitarianism comes down to whether in such predicaments we find it within ourselves to look to the allegedly higher good of aggregate happiness and to tolerate the unequal treatment of individuals. Ronald Dworkin draws a useful distinction between treating people equally, where each gets the same, and treating them as equals, where the claims of each are equally considered, whether or not this means that the people are treated equally. The utilitarian might argue that on his approach individuals are treated as equals, in the sense that the want-satisfaction accruing to each under every dispensation is taken seriously into account. What is worrying, however, is the extent to which such treatment as an equal may devolve on the utilitarian criterion into unequal treatment.

But the trouble is even more deep-seated than this may suggest. The utilitarian interpretation of what it is to treat people as equals is suspect, not just because of a surprising contingency, that aggregate happiness is often maximised by dealing with people unevenly. It is also suspect on the deep structural count, that in respect of many issues some of the wants which individuals have can only be satisfied by the uneven treatment of others. We saw in chapter 11 that the utilitarian will not wish to take account of just every sort of want: in particular he will try to ignore wants which presuppose the acceptance of a non-utilitarian political philosophy and perhaps also non-utilitarian moral wants and wants that have regard to other people. Even the strictest limitation on such wants, however, will allow certain desires to enter the utilitarian calculation that are bound to compromise its egalitarian base. The reason is that if, for example, someone holds by a non-utilitarian political philosophy, say a form of racialism, then the desire which he has for a certain sort of policy will engender within him associated desires that bear only on his own welfare. His racialism may mean that he takes an undue satisfaction in having members of his own ethnic group as colleagues, neighbours or rulers and there is no way that the utilitarian can eliminate the influence of such a disposition on calculations as to what will produce the greatest aggregate happiness. The procedure described in the last chapter would pick up the effects of the disposition, for example, and even the impartial spectator would be hard pressed to define a ground for identifying and ignoring them: how could he know that the desire in question was not spontaneous, rather than the issue of a non-utilitarian conception of justice?

As Ronald Dworkin has been at pains to emphasise, the fact that the utilitarian cannot guard against the influence on his calculations of such externally motivated desires means that the egalitarian claim to treat individuals as equals turns sour on him. People are not properly treated as equals if some of them have desires whose satisfaction specifically demands the unequal treatment of others, and these desires are taken into account as much as are the spontaneous, self-regarding desires to which the utilitarian would like to be able to restrict his attention. It may sometimes be just an unhappy accident that treating people as equals in the utilitarian mould means treating them unequally; at other times, however, it will be more than an accident, stemming from the nature of the desires which the utilitarian is concerned to satisfy.

Let us return for further illustration to our dozen children and the problem of distributing the bag of sweets. It is not unthinkable that there will be some children who will be less happy to receive a sweet each as part of a general distribution than to be left with nothing in a distribution which favours their mates, in the persons of the three oldest children, over other children whom they regard as common rivals and foes. The utilitarian has the problem that he cannot easily ignore such dispositions without giving up altogether the project of maximising want-satisfaction, and that to attend to them is to ensure that the children will be treated unequally. It seems that there is no way that he can cherish utility without paying court to inequality.

The problem can be writ large as well as small. Suppose that a measure is put up for utilitarian referendum, which would have a randomly selected ten per cent of the population perform all menial jobs, domestic and public, at a subsistence level of income. In a questionnaire designed to pick up the expected utility for each individual of such a system, each subject would be asked to give his relative preferences over, say, being in the ten per cent bracket within the proposed regime, being in the ninety per cent bracket, being someone in the existing system who cannot afford to employ domestic help, or being someone who can: these represent the positions available to him or occupied by him under the different dispensations. Undoubtedly he would rank the minority position in the proposed system very low indeed, but presumably he would rank the majority one fairly high: much higher, in all probability, than the position of the majority in the existing system who cannot afford domestic help. And, since the minority position in the novel regime will be weighted for each individual by a fraction of $^1/_{10}$, against a weighting of $^9/_{10}$ for the majority role, it is quite likely that the expected utility for each person of the system involving menial slaves will be higher than the utility attached to the *status quo* by the bulk of the population who cannot afford domestic help. In this case it is also likely that the novel dispensation will turn out to promise a greater social utility than that which is offered by the existing regime and, that being so, the utilitarian can have no option but to recommend that it be instituted.

This illustrates the inegalitarian tendency of the welfare criterion of justice in a circumstance where there is no special problem with the effects on people's desires of political or other aspirations. If such inequality may be sponsored in the green wood, it takes no powerful imagination to see what may be promoted in the dry. In a society where a racial minority are oppressed by the general run of people it will naturally, if unhappily, transpire that many individuals will form personal preferences which reflect this racialism: they will find intolerable the prospect of having to work with, reside near, or take orders from a member of the minority. And if that does indeed transpire, then the utilitarian policy of maximising want-satisfaction, even a policy that ignores directly political preferences, will lead on many issues to the recommendation of inegalitarian resolutions.

The central difficulty then for utilitarianism is that it does not give a guarantee of distributive fairness such as most of us probably feel to be required. It is quite possible, especially in view of the corruption of people's preferences by non-utilitarian philosophies, that a system in which a minority are relatively abused will produce a greater aggregate level of happiness than one in which some plausible distributive constraint governs the allocation of social benefits among individuals. People differ on the question of what principle of distribution ought to operate in a society, whether one of rewarding effort, for example, recognising contribution or regarding need, but most of us would agree that there ought not to be discrimination against any subset of the population on some arbitrary ground such as colour, religion or selection in a random procedure. If someone shares this intuition, as I certainly do, and if he is as unwilling to dismantle it as I am, then he does not have the stomach to be a utilitarian. Justice means something to him other than maximising the satisfaction of people's wants, and he will have to look elsewhere than to utilitarianism for an analysis of it.

The difficulty may prompt the attempt to modify utilitarianism and, as most modifications have it, to produce a mixed criterion of justice: a criterion according to which the just charter is one which maximises want-satisfaction, subject to some further condition. There are many constraints that may plausibly be put on the application of the welfare criterion. One variety might be constructed by borrowing from John Rawls the restriction that he puts on the charters between which there is a political choice to be made. He says that a charter, a set of solutions to the issues of politics outlined in chapter 2, should amount to a conception of right, where this means that the principles it embodies should be general in form, not mentioning particular persons; that they should be universal in application, applying potentially to everyone; and that they should be publicly recognised as the final court of appeal for resolving people's conflicting claims. It is by no means certain that the imposition of this Rawlsian restriction on the utilitarian criterion would guard against the undesired inequalities but the possibility might be worth investigating in another context. A problem which would seem to remain is that even though rival charters satisfy rightness it may be clear to everyone that the effect of one of the charters will be inegalitarian in a particular regard and the perception of this likely result may cause the charter to win on the utilitarian calculation.

A more reliable method of tempering the inegalitarian aspect of the welfare criterion is proposed by Ronald Dworkin. As we mentioned in chapter 11, Dworkin thinks that the best argument for the criterion is that it seems to respect the equality of people: this, in the sense of treating individuals as equals, rather than always treating them equally. He finds fault with the criterion on the particular ground that it cannot restrict itself satisfactorily to people's personal and spontaneous desires: this means, on his view, that the effect of the criterion comes into conflict with its egalitarian motivation, and that a certain inconsistency is produced. The remedy which he proposes is the introduction of proprietarian constraints on the operation of the utilitarian standard. Welfare is to be maximised, subject to the non-infringement of certain rights that belong inalienably to individuals, the rights being the only guarantee that the equality of individuals will be respected.

It is arguable that Dworkin is more faithful than orthodox utilitarians to the tradition stemming from Bentham. The nineteenth-century fathers of the tradition were certainly wedded to egalitarian ideals: witness Bentham's own counsel that each should count for one, and none for more than one. Perhaps the only reason why they did not countenance natural rights as independent constraints on the maximisation of utility was that they failed to perceive the difficulty of focusing utilitarian calculation on to personal and spontaneous preferences. Be that as it may, however, utilitarianism in the unmodified form in which we know it is a criterion of justice with inegalitarian consequences and Dworkin's doctrine must be regarded as a piece of heretical revisionism: it is an attempt to produce a mixed criterion which satisfies the test of reflective equilibrium better than the unadulterated welfare formula.

But apart from imposing conditions on the alternatives presented, or introducing constraints to limit the criterion applied, there is a further method of modifying utilitarianism so as to restrict its inegalitarian consequences. The unmodified utilitarian criterion recommends an aggregate maximisation policy based on people's extended preferences but there is no reason why, taking the same base, we should not propose a policy of ensuring a satisfactory minimum for each individual. We could require that happiness should be maximised only when it has been guaranteed that each person enjoys a given amount of welfare, or we could stipulate that the social scheme chosen from among a set of alternatives should give more happiness to the least favoured position than do the competing schemes. At least in this second form, such a criterion of welfare insurance would be as unmixed as its maximisation counterpart. It would also seem to secure the result of guarding against unwanted inequalities. Probably the only obvious objection to it is that it shifts the emphasis from the promotion of welfare to the protection of equality. As we shall see when we come to the next chapter, it is a first step towards the construal of justice as fairness.

In conclusion it may be worth considering how the unmodified utilitarian might hope to make tolerable the inegalitarian results of his conception of justice. The problem for most of us is that the approach allows one person's happiness to compensate for another's misery and that in this sense, as Rawls puts the matter, it does not take seriously the distinction between persons. If the utilitarian could argue that there was reason to downplay that distinction further than our intuitions suggest, he might succeed in weakening our attachment to the more or less equal treatment of individuals and he might make it possible for us to espouse his doctrine.

There are two avenues along which the utilitarian might seek to advance his argument for downgrading the distinction between individual persons. The one course would have him go for a non-individualistic theory of society, a theory which represented the experiences of individuals as all moments or parts in the single life of a super-individual: here perhaps we can see the opening for a novel collectivistic criterion of justice, a criterion of a sort that we deemed implausible in chapter 5 above. Such a theory, however, we must reject, as indeed it would have been rejected by traditional defenders of utilitarianism, on the grounds that we advanced in chapter 6 against non-individualistic conceptions of social life. So long as we are humanistic in our views of agents and the sources of their actions we cannot contemplate acquiescing in any theory that would make them pawns of super-individual forces.

The other course for the utilitarian would be for him to argue that a single person, among whose different phases we are prepared to allow the propriety of compensation, is really more similar than first appears to a society of individuals, and that if we are willing to permit compensation in the one case we ought also to be ready to allow it in the other. This line has recently been explored by Derek Parfit, who argues that on a view of personal identity which is sufficiently complex to take account of the importance we attach to psychological changes within ourselves, such identity, while in its logic it is all-or-nothing, is in its nature a matter of degrees: just as Tom and Harry may both be equally relatives of mine, though Tom is a brother and Harry a sixth cousin, so *PP* at time *t1* and *PP* at time *t2* may both be equally the same person as me, though *PP* at *t2* is someone to whom I am much more intimately related. On the basis of this observation Parfit proposes that it is only realistic to denigrate the fact of our being the same person over a lifetime to a triviality, and to introduce concepts to allow us to speak of ourselves as a succession of different selves, the boundaries of each self being marked by approximate points of psychological transition. With this move he weakens the contrast between, on the one hand, a society of different persons and, on the other, a single person, for this single person now comes to be seen as a sequence of distinct selves. And the weakening of contrast makes it plausible to say that, if we are prepared to allow compensation between selves, we ought on similar grounds to allow such compensation between persons. In each case one entity is deprived in order that another, in comparatively greater measure, should be benefited.

As Parfit acknowledges, the weakening of contrast is a two-edged sword, for equally it might be given as a reason for thinking that compensation across selves is inappropriate: that we ought never to judge that someone's present misery is worthwhile for the sake of the greater good which will be enjoyed in the far future, presumably by a different self. It is less likely, the utilitarian might urge, that we would give up compensation across selves than that we would accept compensation across persons, and so he may confidently invoke the novel theory of persons in the cause of reinforcing his political disposition. His view will be that over time we are each loose strings of selves and that since introducing distributive constraints in the treatment of selves seems a preposterous idea, we ought to give up altogether a concern with such principles. We should focus solely on the maximisation of the happiness experienced in society, however that is allocated to the selves in whom it is realised.

We cannot say much about Parfit's theory in the present context but there are some points to be made which ensure that the utilitarian will not be left with the last word. It is perfectly possible, and it may even be useful, to invent a concept such as that of a Parfittian self and the non-utilitarian may readily agree that each person is liable to be many such selves in the course of his lifetime. The point which needs adjudication, however, is whether this concept of the self is prior to that of the person in political discussion, so that our concern should be the justice of a charter in relation to selves rather than its justice in respect of persons.

It is not clear what would establish priority in the required sense. Psychologically selves may be prior to persons, since my self is what I perhaps feel myself more intimately to be. On the other hand persons seems to have an ontological priority: I can identify a self only by reference to a person, as so-and-so at such-and-such a time, and the name which I attach to the entity is sustained on the basis of personal identity, not identity of self; a change of heart is not enough to make Richard Nixon someone other than Richard Nixon. Such considerations give contrary counsel then on the matter on which we have to decide. The only recourse seems to be to directly political persuasions: we are forced to judge on whether to give primacy to self or person by reference to the normative effects of the two options. But this move closes the circle, for the utilitarian will argue that primacy should be given to the concept of the self on the grounds that the upshot is in harmony with his inegalitarian commitments, while his opponent will ascribe primacy to the concept of the person for the reason that the result supports his opposite intuitions. The utilitarian cannot hope to win us to his doctrine by appealing to the primacy of selves over persons because the intuitions which the alleged primacy is supposed to dismantle are ones which supply us with good reason for rejecting it.

This may mark an end to our deliberations on utilitarianism. We took up the criticism of the doctrine under the heading of normative output in this chapter, having previously examined its internal organisation and the operation of its criterion. The question before us was whether the theory satisfied the test of reflective equilibrium with our intuitions on particular questions of justice.

We argued that it did not, since the utilitarian measure would in many circumstances prescribe a distribution that discriminated arbitrarily against certain individuals: and this, not just through unhappy accident, but because it could not avoid taking account of certain externally motivated desires. The only prospect for the utilitarian who wishes to convert us to his doctrine, rather than just to propose a modified theory, seemed to be that of dismantling the egalitarian intuitions which most of us feel. We saw that he might try to do this either by arguing for a theory of society which would dissolve people into a single super-individual, or by pressing the case for a view of persons which would depict them as loose strings of selves. We argued, however, that neither path was a promising one and that there was good reason why anyone with egalitarian intuitions should resist the charms of a welfare conception of justice.

Bibliographical note

Nicholas Rescher has an extended account of the conflict between utilitarian and egalitarian considerations in *Distributive Justice*, Bobbs-Merrill, New York, 1966. Those interested in the general topic of equality should consult Albert Weale, *Equality*, Routledge & Kegan Paul, London, 1978. Dworkin's distinction between equal treatment and treatment as equal, plus his case for a utilitarianism modified by proprietarian constraints, is made in *Taking Rights Seriously*, Duckworth, London, 1968, chapters 9 and 12. David Braybrooke also argues for the tempering of an immediate appeal to welfare by a recognition of certain rights but unlike Dworkin he thinks that these rights are grounded in a longer-term invocation of welfare: Dworkin regards equality as the common base both for regarding welfare and respecting rights. See Braybrooke, *Three Tests for Democracy*, Random House, New York, 1968. Rawls's account of the constraints of right on a charter, such as might be introduced in a modification of utilitarianism, is to be found in *A Theory of Justice*, Oxford University Press, 1972, pp. 130–6. His criticism of utilitarianism for not taking seriously the distinction between persons is presented in the same work, pp. 22–33. Robert Nozick invokes the same consideration as an argument against any non-proprietarian conception of justice in *Anarchy, State and Utopia*, Blackwell, London, Oxford, 1974; see his argument, summarised in chapter 10 above, for the right of each individual not to be sacrificed for the benefit of others. R. B. Perry, *General Theory of Value*, Longmans Green, New York, 1926, suggests the connection between utilitarianism and a non-individualistic theory of society. Derek Parfit mentions the possibility of a utilitarian's helping himself to a novel view of persons in 'Later Selves and Moral Principles', in Alan Monte-fiore, ed., *Philosophy and Personal Relations*, Routledge & Kegan Paul, London, 1973.

Part V The contractarian criterion of justice

14   Justice as fairness

It appears that the concept of welfare does not do any better than that of legitimacy in giving us an explication of what constitutes the justice of a social charter. In this chapter we turn to a third attempt to analyse what it is that should guide us in distinguishing just resolutions to political issues from unjust ones, and in isolating that overall arrangement of social matters which is to stand as our ultimate ideal. The criterion offered in this case identifies social justice with fairness, a concept which it construes in a highly distinctive, although not idiosyncratic manner. The conception of justice as fairness comes directly from the contemporary American philosopher, John Rawls, but as Rawls himself maintains, it has deeper historical roots, particularly in the work of the eighteenth-century German thinker, Immanuel Kant. Where Nozick can be seen as revamping the ideas of the seventeenth-century philosopher, John Locke, in the attempt to develop an alternative political philosophy to utilitarianism, Rawls can be viewed as updating some of Kant's insights to a similar purpose: on this picture utilitarianism is the common, dominant foe, and it is more or less incidental that proprietarianism and contractarianism come into conflict with each other on separate counts.

But whatever of its Kantian roots, the immediate background to the development of the contractarian criterion is to be found in the history of welfare thinking among economists from the rejection of utilitarianism in the 1930s. It will be recalled that in that decade many economists came to believe that utilities could not be assigned satisfactory cardinal or comparable measures: this mistakenly, as we suggested in the chapter before last. In the decades following, welfare economists struggled to formulate an alternative standard of economic progress and it will be useful to review the story of that struggle if we are to understand the significance of Rawls's proposal.

Initially, the favoured alternative to utilitarianism was a criterion adopted from the late nineteenth-century Italian economist and sociologist, Vilfredo Pareto. The Pareto criterion lays down two rules: (1) that if everyone in a society is indifferent between two systems *S'* and *S''*, the society ought to be indifferent too; and (2) that if at least one individual prefers *S'* to *S''*, and the others are at worst indifferent – i.e. no one has the opposite preference – the society ought to prefer *S'* to *S''* also. The criterion is appealing because it does not require that we be able to measure or compare the intensities of the individuals' preferences, only that we know what the preferences are. The stipulation that social indifference follow on individual indifference, and that the preference of even one person dictate social preference if all the others are indifferent, seems impossible to resist. If a criterion of social welfare failed to incorporate it we should certainly conclude that something was wrong.

The problem with the Pareto criterion, it turns out, is not that there is anything objectionable about this stipulation, but that the criterion does not go any further. Consider a situation where a population has to choose between three alternatives, *x, y* and *z*. It may be that *x* and *y* both prove to be Pareto-superior to *z*, at least one person preferring each to *z* and no one preferring *z* to either *x* or *y*. Thus the criterion has told us that on no account is *z* to be considered for social implementation. But what will it tell us about *x* and *y*? Well, if it happens that one person in the population prefers *x* to *y* and another *y* to *x*, then it will tell us nothing. Both are Pareto-optimal, as is sometimes said, in the sense that there is no alternative that is Pareto-superior to either. As to which of them is better, however, the criterion gives us no information. We must look elsewhere if we are to find reason for arguing that one or other ought to be socially preferred.

This feature of the Pareto criterion is sometimes described as its incompleteness, the complete criterion being one which says something about any two alternatives up for consideration: that the one is better than the other, or that they are equally good or bad. It is a grave lack for the reason that in most cases of assessing competing systems there will be some clash of individuals' preferences. Thus the Pareto criterion would fail to designate an egalitarian utopia as better than a severely hierarchical *status quo* in which most people live at starvation level, on the grounds that one or two rich individuals prefer to leave things as they are.

The incompleteness of the Pareto criterion led welfare economists to consider various amendments and alternatives. The amendments proposed came generally to be criticised, and inevitably attention was focused on the possibility of alternatives. Here a natural candidate was something which we may call the social decision criterion. According to a social decision criterion one option facing a population is better than another if, using a particular voting procedure, it would be chosen by members of the population. There are as many decision criteria as there are voting procedures but it would not seem to be difficult to narrow down the range of acceptable procedures. The most natural procedure to suggest is that of majority decision, which would designate one option as superior to another if a majority of the population vote for it. Thus we get the political philosophy – or the welfare economics – of majoritarianism.

The resort to a social decision criterion such as majoritarianism must have a certain appeal for us, not so much because it avoids the calculation and comparison of utilities, but more because it takes the distinction between persons more seriously than utilitarianism. With such a criterion, each person's vote counts as heavily as those of his fellows and no one is asked to accept relative deprivation in order to secure a comparatively greater amelioration in the condition of another. The difference between the philosophies can be nicely brought out if we imagine applying them to determine where three friends who want to holiday together should actually go. Suppose that two of the friends prefer Spain to any of the relevant alternatives, but that the third has a very much more intense preference for Italy over Spain, Italy being, say, the second best liked alternative for the others. In such a case majoritarianism would prescribe Spain, giving each person equal say, but the possibility is that utilitarianism, allowing for the comparative intensities of preference, would recommend Italy.

Majoritarianism, or indeed any plausible decision criterion, turns out to have as many problems as its utilitarian counterpart. One of these concerns its operation or applicability, another its acceptability or outcome: the first had an important influence among welfare economists, although the second must probably seem more serious to us. The applicability problem was rigorously demonstrated in the early 1950s by the American economist Kenneth Arrow. In his so-called impossibility theorem Arrow showed that there was no voting procedure satisfying certain loose conditions of acceptability which was proof against producing an irrational result. In other words, for every such procedure there was a possible pattern of voting which would give an inconsistent result: say, a choice of A over B, of B over C and, impossibly, of C over A. The conditions which Arrow proposed that a procedure must satisfy are: the condition of unrestricted domain, that the procedure work for any pattern of voting; the weak Pareto condition, that if everyone prefers x to y then x will be selected by the procedure; the dictatorship condition, that no individual's vote should automatically be decisive; and the condition of the independence of irrelevant alternatives. This last condition is that if a society is choosing between x, y and z then which option is selected should only be determined by the individuals' ranking of the alternatives *vis-à-vis* one another; it should not be determined in any way, for example, by how they rank, x, y and z against an irrelevant alternative w, so that if their ranking against w changed so might their selection from among x, y and z. It is worth mentioning that this condition is broken by the utilitarian criterion, as we elaborated this in the chapter before last, for when we are considering someone's utility function over four options A, B, C and D, we shall alter the place assigned to any one of them on the person's scale of relative intensities if we introduce a fifth option at the top or bottom of the scale.

Rather than reproducing Arrow's proof of his theorem here, we may satisfy ourselves by providing an illustration of it. The best known example of a voting procedure's producing an irrational result is given in the so-called 'paradox of voting' which had already been fully characterised in the nineteenth century. Suppose that we have three individuals who want to decide, by the method of majority voting, between three alternative arrangements A, B and C. Imagine now that person 1 prefers A to B to C, person 2, B to C to A and person 3, C to A to B. Consider what would happen in such a case. A would be socially preferred to B, receiving two votes against B's one, and B would be preferred to C, receiving in its turn two votes against C's one. It ought to follow that A is preferred to C, the transitivity which allows us to deduce this from the fact that A is preferred to B and B to C being part of any rational set of choices. But this is not in fact what happens. For if we examine the voting pattern again we shall see that C gets two votes against A's one, thus giving us the 'cyclical' or 'intransitive' pattern that A is preferred to B, B to C and C to A.

But the technical difficulty of defining a satisfactory voting procedure is not the only problem which faces a political philosophy such as majoritarianism. Perhaps more important is the fact that like utilitarianism it looks incapable of securing the distributive balance which intuitively we wish to see realised in any political system that we are going to defend. With utilitarianism the failure of balance came of the fact that the philosophy would allow the benefit attained by some to compensate for deprivation suffered by others, and this up to extremes. With majoritarianism it derives from the possibility of bias and self-interest determining how people vote. Such bias may ensure, for example, that a minority will be consistently discriminated against in the ordering of a society: the tyranny of a majority is no textbook imagining but a state of affairs illustrated in everyday life. And if we felt unable to espouse utilitarianism because it might force us to approve of arbitrary discrimination against a minority, we must resist the charms of majoritarianism on exactly the same grounds. We cannot take to ourselves a philosophy which would countenance rank discrimination.

Rawls's contractarian proposal may be viewed as the next significant stage in the history of this non-utilitarian tradition of thought. What produces the possibility of discrimination in the case of utilitarianism is that the approach does not take seriously the distinction between persons, a feature which is put right in a social decision criterion such as majoritarianism. However, majoritarianism fails itself on the same count, although now because of a different characteristic: that it allows self-interest and bias to influence the votes which people cast for rival schemes. The contractarian criterion is the natural successor of this majoritarian one, for what it attempts to do is to go one stage further and to remedy in turn the feature which causes trouble in the social decision approach. The proposal which it embodies is that the just social scheme is that which answers to people's preferences, but not now the preferences recorded in a regular voting procedure: rather the preferences which people would have over alternative social arrangements, were they not influenced by self-interest and bias.

In discussing the individualistic nature of our sense of justice in chapter 5 we saw that a social scheme is regarded by us as just to the extent that it fulfils the interests of individuals. The different political philosophies that we have been considering put variant constructions on the interests to which social arrangements are supposed to answer. The proprietarian claims to discover them in the so-called natural rights of individuals, the utilitarian in the extended preferences of people over alternative social arrangements, the majoritarian in people's recorded preferences in respect of such rival dispensations, and the contractarian in the enlightened preferences that individuals have over the competing schemes. We found fault with natural rights for being internally obscure, and for tolerating inherited privilege and deprivation; with extended preferences, at least when they are tied to maximisation policy, for allowing compensation across people that could mean serious inequality; and with recorded preferences for reflecting bias and self-interest in a manner likely to allow discrimination against a minority. The hope of the contractarian is that

147

the enlightened preferences of individuals, the preferences which they would have were they disinterested and unbiased, will serve as a more compelling index of the interests which we think that a just social charter ought to satisfy.

There are a number of ways in which one might conceivably try to retrieve people's enlightened preferences, working out what they would vote for, were they free from the influence of self-interest and bias. The impartial spectator technique favoured by some utilitarians, for example, might be thought to isolate one's own extended preferences, albeit preferences directed by a concern to maximise welfare: this technique was mentioned briefly at the end of the chapter before last. Rawls's contractarianism is distinguished, however, not just by its focus on people's enlightened preferences, but by the formula proposed for extricating those preferences. The formula is that an individual's enlightened preference in regard to a set of social schemes is that preference which it would be rational for him to adopt, assuming that he is concerned with his own welfare, were he in ignorance of what position he would occupy under any of the candidate schemes. The scheme which ought to be chosen by the society then, the scheme which satisfies the enlightened preferences of the individuals involved, is that which those individuals or their representatives would agree to if they were forced to negotiate a choice under such conditions of ignorance. The idea, and it surely has a powerful intuitive appeal, is that the rational concern with one's own interest under appropriate circumstances of ignorance will be tantamount to a concern that is free from the usual warping effect of egoism and bias: it will be a concern for the position of everyone, since the ignorance stipulation ensures that one must allow for the possibility of being in every position that anyone occupies.

Contractarianism gets its name from the device which it uses to filter out people's enlightened preferences. It postulates an ideal situation for casting votes and seeks to identify the choice that would be made there among alternative social charters: the social contract, as it is often said, that those casting the votes would establish with one another. The postulated contract has certain affinities with the option for socio-political organisation which seventeenth century theorists took to mark the transition from the state of nature, but here it plays an entirely different role. There is no suggestion that the actual social system is legitimate in so far as it rests on an implicit contract, whether or not realised in history. The idea of the contract is not to legitimate what exists but to give us a means of working out what ought to exist. It is argued that while we cannot attach ourselves to what people would choose politically in their regular circumstances, we may be able to espouse what they would choose in circumstances designed to eliminate the effects of self-interest and bias. And if we are to work out what they would choose under such conditions we cannot help but trade in the currency of the fictional social contract.

The situation of ignorance in which the contractarian contemplates people coming to political resolutions is described by Rawls as the original position of contract. In the remainder of this chapter I mean to spell out the main features of this position but first it may be useful to give a summary quotation from Rawls himself.

> I assume that the parties are situated behind a veil of ignorance. They do not know how the various alternatives will affect their own particular case and they are obliged to evaluate principles solely on the basis of general considerations. . . . First of all, no one knows his place in society, his class position or social status; nor does he know his fortune in the distribution of natural assets and abilities, his intelligence and strength, and the like. Nor again, does anyone know his conception of the good, the particulars of his rational plan of life, or even the special features of his psychology such as his aversion to risk or liability to optimism or pessimism. More than this, I assume that the parties do not know the particular circumstances of their own society. . . . It is taken for granted, however, that they know the general facts about human society. They understand political affairs and the principles of economic theory; they know the basis of social organisation and the laws of human psychology. Indeed, the parties are presumed to know whatever general facts affect the choice of the principles of justice. (*A Theory of Justice*, henceforth TJ, pp. 136–7)

There are four questions that must be answered even in a brief characterisation of the original position imagined by Rawls. They are: (1) 'Who chooses?'; (2) 'What is chosen?'; (3) 'With what knowledge?'; and (4) 'With what motivation?' In what follows I shall present Rawls's responses to these queries, usually without much discussion of why he takes one line rather than another. Where an answer is found surprising, and I offer no account of it, the explanation is to be found in considerations of reflective equilibrium. It must be remembered that Rawls, most explicitly of all, is committed to the methodology described in chapter four above, and in particular that he wants his criterion of justice to generate concrete assessments of social arrangements that are more or less in line with his intuitive judgments. He is not above designing his representation of the original position in order to ensure such reflective equilibrium; indeed, subject perhaps to the limitation that the criterion should also satisfy intuitive constraints of a more general kind, he thinks that stacking the pack in this way is of the essence of reflective method.

The first question on our agenda is: 'Who chooses?' Rawls's answer to this is, not institutional persons but only individuals, and not individuals in just their own name, but individuals considered as having close family sympathies, in particular sympathies with their descendants (TJ, pp. 128, 145). The main reason for this latter stipulation has to do with issues in intergenerational justice, but we shall see a further motivation for it in the next chapter. The people in the original position then (for short, and henceforth, the POP's) may be seen as the representatives of continuing family lines. Moreover, although this point is only relevant to intergenerational matters, the POP's are all drawn from a single generation (TJ, p. 140). Somewhat surprisingly, however, Rawls denies that they are an assembly of all the people living at a given time, even of all the people above the age of reason: to imagine that they were such an assembly, he says, would be to stretch fantasy too far (TJ, p. 139). One of the reasons the denial is surprising is that the matter turns out in any case to be unimportant. For as Rawls goes on to emphasise, it is immaterial how many POP's there are since all can be expected to vote in the same way, each being assumed to be equally ignorant and equally rational. 'It is clear that since the differences among the parties are unknown to them, and everyone is equally rational and similarly situated, each is convinced by the same arguments. Therefore, we can view the choice in the original position from the standpoint of one person selected at random' (TJ, p. 139). This means in effect that the answer to the question of who chooses is: you do. What each of us has to ask is how he would vote in the original position, since each of us can assume that others would vote similarly. The exercise is less daunting than it may at first have seemed. 'The veil of ignorance makes possible a unanimous choice of a particular conception of justice. Without these limitations on knowledge the bargaining problem of the original position would be hopelessly complicated' (TJ, p. 140). (Notice that Rawls uses the phrase 'conception of justice' both for a criterion of justice, the usage to which we put the phrase, and for the social charter which that criterion selects as optimal.)

The second question which we have to resolve is: 'What is chosen?' The answer, to sum up a number of elements, is: a charter satisfying the constraints of right, which is meant to govern the society of a people with a sense of justice, under the typical circumstances of justice. That it is a total charter that is to be chosen, rather than the resolution to one or another particular issue, seems to be implicit in Rawls's avowal that he is concerned more with ideal than non-ideal theory (TJ, pp. 8–9, 245–8). Ideal theory, among other restrictions, is not designed to say how existing injustices may be partly remedied; its interest is in specifying the outline only of the perfectly just society. Presumably it may be that the resolution of a given issue, which would be chosen as part of a charter for the just society, is not that which ought to be adopted in the context of an existing society which already contains certain injustices. The matter, however, is not entirely clear and sometimes Rawls suggests that for practical purposes we can also use the contractarian device to work out questions of justice relative to a specific context.

> Viewing the theory of justice as a whole, the ideal part presents a conception of the just society that we are to achieve if we can. Existing institutions are to be judged in the light of this conception and held to be unjust to the extent that they depart from it without sufficient reason. . . . Thus while the principles of justice belong to the theory of an ideal state of affairs, they are generally relevant. (TJ, p. 246)

The charter chosen in the original position is to satisfy the constraints of right. We have seen already what these constraints are, for in the last chapter we held out the possibility that utilitarianism might be suitably modified by their imposition on the alternatives that are up for adjudication. They mean, in a few words, that the principles embodied in the charter must be general in form, that they must be universal in application and that they are to constitute a public, an effective and a definitive means of resolving the conflicts that arise between members of the society (TJ, pp. 130–6).

Finally, the charter chosen is to govern the society of a people with a sense of justice, under the typical circumstances of justice. That the people have a sense of justice means that they are likely to accept a social order that would have been chosen in the original position, even if it is one under which they are allocated a relatively less well-off role: this, assuming that the order was not chosen in disregard of the general facts of human psychology (TJ, p. 145). In treating his enterprise as ideal theory Rawls makes the strong assumption that everyone will comply with the charter adopted but even when this is weakened, and the issues of how to punish non-compliance are raised, people are still taken generally to have a sense of justice (TJ, pp. 575–7). That the society governed by the charter exists under the typical circumstances of justice means that the situation is of that familiar kind which ensures that political questions arise: 'mutually disinterested persons put forward conflicting claims to the division of social advantages under conditions of moderate scarcity' (TJ, p. 128). The circumstances are not those of a monastery, since people lack altruistic commitment; they are not those of an eden, since goods are in relatively short supply. On the other hand the situation is not one of breadline subsistence for, as Rawls says in another connection, 'the parties know that the conditions of their society, whatever they are, admit the effective realisation of equal liberties' (TJ, p. 152).

The third question on our agenda bears on the knowledge with which the POP's have to make their choice of charter. Here the most important point, and it is sufficiently annotated in the initial quotation from Rawls on the original position, is that the parties are under a veil of ignorance about most particular facts concerning themselves and their society. Whatever exceptions there are can be derived from the following stipulation of knowledge, a stipulation that is only implicit in Rawls's own work: that the POP's know of all the facts mentioned above in specifying who chooses and what is chosen. The final point to be made about the cognitive resources of the parties in the original position, and it is also explicit in the quotation from Rawls, is that the parties know whatever general facts affect the choice of social charter, in particular the facts available from the psychological and social sciences. It is not clear whether they are supposed even to know of facts at present undiscovered, but the question is immaterial since, in replicating the judgments which they would make, we can only imagine them to be in possession of facts with which we are ourselves familiar.

This takes us to the fourth and last question on our list: that which concerns the motivation with which the POP's make their choice. There are three points to be made about the motivation of the parties: the first concerns the ends which they pursue, the second the means by which they pursue them and the third a special condition that Rawls imposes on the people's dispositions. As to the ends pursued, the distinctive thing about the original position is that the POP's do not know anything about their particular desires: this, by the veil of ignorance condition. The contractors are thus supposed to choose a social charter, not out of concern for individually variable goals, but out of concern for desires which they are bound to have, regardless of who they are. These are described as general desires (TJ, p. 263), or desires for primary goods (TJ, p. 93): they are meant to be desires for conditions required for the pursuit of any particular goals. Rawls maintains that the primary goods are certain rights and liberties, opportunities and powers, income and wealth and – something assumed to be made possible in the realisation of the others – self-respect (TJ, p. 92). These ends are pursued by each POP as something he wants for himself and those he represents but the parties, it should be remarked, are unconcerned with one another's goals: for simplicity's sake they are assumed in this sense to be mutually disinterested (TJ, p. 129).

As to the means adopted in pursuit of these ends, the parties are assumed to follow the usual guidelines of rationality, as these are described in decision theory.

> Thus, in the usual way, a rational person is thought to have a coherent set of preferences between the options open to him. He ranks these options according to how well they further his purposes; he follows the plan which will satisfy more of his desires rather than less, and which has the greater chance of being successfully executed. (TJ, p. 143)

Here Rawls gives us three principles which he thinks of as guiding rational choice: the principles of effective means, inclusiveness and greater likelihood (TJ, pp. 411–12). In the next chapter we shall see something more of what he takes rationality to entail, but in the meantime it should just be noticed that he takes the condition of deliberative rationality to be met by the POP's (TJ, pp. 416–24). This means that in choosing their charter the parties consider all the predictable consequences of the plan and that they balance these against the foreseen consequences of the alternatives: they act, so far as possible, in a manner for which they cannot afterwards reproach themselves.

Finally, the special condition which Rawls imposes on the motivation of the parties in the original position is that in making his choice none of them is influenced by envy. 'He is not ready to accept a loss for himself if only others have less as well' (TJ, p. 143). This is not psychologically realistic, for undoubtedly we are most of us afflicted by envy from time to time. Rawls feels that he may be permitted the assumption on the grounds: first, that to allow envy would be to open the possibility of a collectively disadvantageous system's being chosen in the original position; and second, that the system which is actually selected by the contractarian criterion, the system described in the next chapter, is unlikely to generate strong feelings of envy itself (TJ, p. 144; on the second claim see also TJ, pp. 534–41).

This completes our initial account of the contractarian criterion of justice. We began this chapter with a consideration of the lines explored among welfare economists after the rejection of utilitarianism in the 1930s. We saw that they first toyed with the Pareto criterion but that due to the incompleteness of this measure attention moved to various social decision criteria, in particular the majoritarian one. However, this proved to have its problems too: the technical one analysed in Arrow's impossibility theorem and, more important for us, the normative problem of condoning the tyranny of a majority. We presented Rawls's contractarian criterion as an amendment of this majoritarian candidate which replaced people's recorded preferences with their enlightened ones: that is, with the preferences which they would have, were they free from self-interest and bias. The device used by Rawls for extricating such enlightened preferences is that of the original position, with the problem of choice that it presents to would-be social contractors, and in the last part of the chapter we answered four questions related to this position: (1) 'Who chooses?'; (2) 'What is chosen?'; (3) 'With what knowledge?'; and (4) 'With what motivation?'.

Bibliographical note

The classic attack on utilitarianism from within welfare economics is Lionel Robbins, *An Essay on the Nature and Significance of Economic Science*, Macmillan, London, 1932. For an account of the Pareto criterion, and the various amendments to which it was subjected, see Amartya Sen, *Collective Choice and Social Welfare*, Oliver & Boyd, London, 1970, chapters 2 and 2*. Arrow's theorem is informally presented in Kenneth Arrow's 'Values and Decision-Making', in Peter Laslett and W. G. Runciman, eds, *Philosophy, Politics and Society*, Cambridge University Press, 1967, and it is fully discussed in Sen, op. cit., chapters 3 and 3*. On the placing of Rawls's criterion in relation to utilitarian and majoritarian approaches see Sen, chapters 9 and 9*. Sen also has interesting and relevant remarks in his paper 'Informational Analysis of Moral Principles', in Ross Harrison, ed., *Rational Action*, Cambridge University Press, 1979. Rawls discusses the Kantian roots of his theory in 'A Kantian Conception of Equality', in *Cambridge Review*, vol. 96, no. 2225, 1975. For the other aspects of his theory see *A Theory of Justice*, Oxford University Press, 1972. D. A. J. Richards adopts an explicitly Rawlsian approach to ethical, as distinct from political, matters in *A Theory of the Reasons for Action*, Oxford University Press, 1971. This is worth consulting for the slightly variant presentation of the original position and for the very full discussion of the rationality of POP's. Before publishing *A Theory of Justice*, Rawls had presented initial sketches of his point of view in various articles. For an account of the development of his thought through these articles see Robert Paul Wolff, *Understanding Rawls*, Princeton University Press, 1977, chapters 4–8. Wolff also has a discussion of the Kantian precedent to Rawls's theory in chapters 10–12.

15   The demands of fairness

When we were dealing with proprietarianism we saw that by means of Nozick's moral-cum-rational derivation it was possible to isolate the charter which a legitimacy criterion would tend to favour. This identification of a favoured charter we found to be out of the question with utilitarianism: which arrangement was to be selected by the welfare criterion depended on the wants of the population and was liable to vary from one society to another. We now have to explore the question with contractarianism of whether there is a convincing argument whereby the fairness criterion can be linked with a specific charter, a charter which it will pick out as best for any population. Rawls takes a strongly positive line on the matter, arguing that to espouse fairness as the form of social justice is in substance to adopt an equally distinctive proposal for the organisation of society, a proposal which he characterises in his famous two principles. Our main task in this chapter will be to analyse the contractarian case which Rawls makes for this two-principles charter.

To argue in the contractarian manner for the adoption of a charter is to urge that the charter is that which it would be rational for the parties in the original position to choose. Such a claim can be defended by consideration of the line of reasoning which a party picked at random is likely to follow: since each person in the position is equally ignorant and equally rational, it must be assumed that each will be moved by the same pattern of argument (TJ, p. 139). Taking the point of view of that randomly selected party we have to ask two questions: first, which strategy of choice is he going to adopt, and second, which alternative scheme is he then going to favour. But the questions may also be put in the first person and made the more engaging. What each of us has to do in order to see where the fairness criterion of justice leads is to ask how we would choose, and what we would choose, were we to find ourselves within the original position.

The problem of strategy, to take up the first question, is acutely raised by the original position because the choice situation is one of uncertainty. Each POP is presented with a number of alternative charters and is required to make an option from among them but he is left in the dark with regard to the consequence that any choice will have for him personally. He is uncertain where he will end up within the social system that he happens to choose, whether among the upper echelons or in the lower dregs. This means that each option before him, each charter for the organisation of society, has the character of a gamble so far as he is concerned: seizing upon it, he may yet find himself with any one of a number of possible outcomes. The predicament is parallel to the various cases of choice under uncertainty which one finds described in textbooks on decision theory. For example, it may be likened to the situation where one has to decide whether to go out to the cinema for the evening, despite being unsure about the quality of the film; whether to go to the library to work, although one does not know if any relevant book will be available; or whether to venture down the road to the local pub, in ignorance as to the possibility of joining up with a friend or acquaintance. In this case, as in that with which we are concerned, each option is associated with a number of different possible outcomes, and the person choosing does not know which outcome is liable to be realised in the event of his picking a particular option.

The problem of strategy is sharpened by the uncertainty under which the POP's must choose, because there is little consensus among decision theorists as to the demands of rationality in such a case. Roughly distinguished, there are three possible strategies of choice available under uncertainty: further refined approaches are described in the literature, but it is unnecessary to explore them here. They may be respectively characterised as the strategies of the optimist, the pessimist and the gambler. The optimist's approach is to take that option whose best outcome is the best of all: being optimistic, he is sure enough of attaining the outcome not to worry about the other possibilities. This strategy is described as the maximax one, since it means going for the maximum among the maxima, the best outcome among the best outcomes. The pessimist's approach, by sharp contrast, is to go for that option whose worst outcome is the best of the worst outcomes possible: being pessimistic, he is convinced that he will get the worst outcome for any alternative chosen and so he ignores the other outcomes that may eventuate. This strategy is described as the maximin one, since it means pursuing the maximum of the minima, the best outcome among the worst outcomes. Finally, the gambler's approach is to try to take all the outcomes into account for each option before him, putting a probability figure on the chance of each coming about if the option is chosen and using these figures as a base for maximising expected utility. It will be recalled from chapter 12 above that to maximise expected utility as between two options A and B, where each can have either of two outcomes, A1 or A2 and B1 or B2, is to choose that option whose outcomes yield the highest figure, when their respective utilities are weighted by the associated probabilities and added to one another. The expected utility of A, for example, will be $P(A1)U(A1) + P(A2)U(A2)$, where $P(A1)$ is the probability of A1 coming about if A is chosen, and $U(A1)$ is the utility of A1 to the agent. A will be adopted by the gambler in preference to B if this sum is greater than $P(B1)U(B1) + P(B2)U(B2)$.

Should our randomly selected POP maximax, maximin or maximise expected utility? That is the problem of strategy which calls to be resolved in applying the contractarian criterion of justice. We can say with some confidence straight off that it would not be rational for a POP to maximax, for this optimistic approach leaves open the possibility that the person will get the worst outcome of all and does so without offering any balance of assurance that a better outcome is more likely. It counsels the wild and wanton course of staking everything on the unknown chance of striking the jackpot, a course which it is natural to deem irrational and which orthodox decision theory unites in denouncing.

But what of the decision as between maximinning and maximising expected utility? There is no consensus as to which of these strategies it is rational to follow under uncertainty and our intuitions are scarcely unambiguous on the issue. There seems to be a great deal of sense in playing safe, as the maximin rule would have one do, but it may be argued on the other hand that this is excessively pessimistic and that one should take all the outcomes possible into account, in the fashion of the person who maximises expected utility, not concentrate exclusively on the worst outcome that may eventuate. In order to maximise expected utility, of course, the agent must be able to assign probabilities to the different outcomes possible for each option but even where he is ignorant of the relevant determining factors he can do this by applying the principle of insufficient reason, assigning the same probability to each of the results that may come about on the choice of a given option: each is held to be equally probable since there is no reason sufficient for thinking otherwise.

In the application of his contractarian criterion Rawls argues that the rational course for each of the POP's in the original position is to maximin and he offers three reasons for thinking that this is so (TJ, pp. 154–6). Two of the reasons have to do with the precise relation between the two-principles charter and the alternatives: the first is that the minimum that the charter offers is quite satisfactory, and the second that the minima of the alternatives are wholly intolerable. If we assume for the moment that this is indeed so, then it must be granted that the two considerations are powerful reasons for adopting the maximin strategy. For why should one risk ending up with an intolerable outcome in the hope of achieving something better than an outcome that is already satisfactory? If the scenario is as Rawls describes it, then the maximin rule must make a compelling claim to be the rational strategy of choice.

Rawls's third reason for thinking that rationally each of the POP's ought to maximin is that on which he seems to place greatest weight. He argues that from behind the veil of ignorance a person cannot estimate in a satisfactory way the probability of his ending up in one or another position within the social system for which he opts. He may make a rough guess but that is scarcely a sound basis on which to make an important choice: and a choice, at that, which he must be able to justify to his descendants as well as to himself.

> The veil of ignorance excludes all but the vaguest knowledge of likelihoods. The parties have no basis for determining the probable nature of their society, or their place in it. Thus they have strong reasons for being wary of probability calculations if any other course is open to them. They must also take into account the fact that their choice of principles should seem reasonable to others, in particular their descendants, whose rights will be deeply affected by it. (TJ, p. 155)

This argument shows that, without adverting to the fact, Rawls adopts one of two perfectly feasible interpretations of what the veil of ignorance involves. The veil of ignorance requires, by way of eliminating the effects of bias and self-interest, that the POP should not know which position in any given system he is liable to occupy, if that system receives his vote: to partition positions rather roughly, for example, he does not know whether he will end up among the bottom third, the middle third, or the top third. This requirement would be fulfilled were the POP to be told that his position in the system would be determined by random allocation: people would pick straws to establish their social stations. Rawls rejects the thin veil of ignorance which this allocation would entail, for on the story told there is a clear objective probability which the POP can assign to each of the available positions within the system chosen: the probability is the same for each position, assuming that positions are occupied by the same number of people, since the allocation of people to positions is random.

The interpretation of the veil of ignorance which Rawls adopts makes it into a thick veil. He supposes that the POP is told, not that his position in the system chosen will be assigned by random allocation, but that it will be determined by his own talent, effort and fortune. This means that the objective probability of the person getting into any position in the system is beyond his cognitive reach, since he is ignorant of what his own properties are. He knows that each person may have a different probability of getting into the position, since he knows that people vary in their properties, but he has no idea which probability applies in his own case. The ignorance under which he labours is no gentle twilight, but a Stygian gloom.

But even if we accept Rawls's thick veil of ignorance as the reasonable one to draw over the original position, we may wonder whether it really follows that the POP's should spurn probability calculations. After all, might a person not reasonably apply the principle of insufficient reason under the thick veil and argue that for any given system he has an equal chance, say, of getting into the bottom, middle or top third of the population? True, any one of these thirds may be internally differentiated: the most of those in the top third, for example, may be very much less well-off than the 5 per cent elite. But the POP will be able to work out such possibilities, and allow for them, within the original position, since he has access to general facts about social life, such as the facts about the inequalities occasioned by different sorts of regime. In any case Rawls himself envisages that the POP may consider applying the principle of insufficient reason and assigning probabilities on the basis of it. 'He assumes that there is an equal likelihood of his turning out to be anyone, fully endowed with that person's preferences, abilities, and social position' (TJ, p. 165).

But apart from dropping a thick rather than a thin veil over the original position, Rawls maintains that it would be unreasonable of a POP to appeal in the manner described to the principle of insufficient reason. He thinks that the probabilities in which any important decision is based should always be derived from a knowledge of specific facts, and in particular that they should have this status if the decision has to be justified to others.

I have simply assumed that judgments of probability, if they are to be grounds of rational decision, must have an objective basis, that is, a basis in knowledge of particular facts (or in reasonable beliefs). This evidence need not take the form of reports of relative frequencies but it should provide grounds for estimating the relative strength of the various tendencies that affect the outcome. The necessity for objective reasons is all the more urgent in view of the fundamental significance of the choice in the original position and the fact that the parties want their decision to appear well founded to others. (TJ, pp. 172–3)

In this latter comment on the justification of the decision to others we see once again an appeal to the fact that the POP's are representatives of continuing lines and not individuals acting in their own name. Elsewhere it is more explicit when Rawls makes this comment on the assumption that the POP's would not apply the principle of insufficient reason. 'This supposition is plausible in view of the fundamental importance of the original agreement and the desire to have one's decision appear responsible to one's descendants who will be affected by it' (TJ, p. 169).

So much then for Rawls's argument that the problem of strategy would be resolved by each POP in favour of the maximin approach. The second question concerns the alternative which would be favoured by a POP of a maximinning mentality. Among the charters presented for the contemplation of the parties in the original position, which will best seem to guarantee the social station of the worst off person? In examining this question Rawls adopts a disappointing tactic, which is to consider his two-principles charter only in the context of what he calls a shorter list of alternatives. The list is made up of the two-principles charter itself, a number of variations on that charter, and finally some charters that directly transcribe traditional criteria of justice as principles for organising social life (TJ, pp. 122–6, see also pp. 65–75).

This last category of alternatives can be dealt with first. Take the utilitarian criterion of justice, a criterion which Rawls thinks it is more reasonable to read in the average rather than the aggregate sense: this, because he is concerned with intergenerational issues, and in particular population policy, where it makes a difference which view one takes. Rawls assimilates this criterion to the charter which would have a society solve its political issues, and if necessary continually adjust its solutions, so as to ensure the maximisation of average happiness. The approach marks a divergence from the way of thinking maintained in this book, for on our account of utilitarianism the concern with happiness may lead one to adopt a charter which itself makes no mention of that

161

guiding value, but merely stipulates a certain pattern of solutions to political issues. Rawls's utilitarian, like ours, recommends something which can be called a utilitarian charter. For Rawls, however, that means a charter which lays down as the rule for governing social life, and it will be a rule satisfying the constraints of right, the principle that utility must always be maximised, whereas for us it means any charter, any set of political solutions, which promises to produce maximum utility, so far as the matter can be judged at present. 'Utilitarianism, as I have defined it,' Rawls says, 'is the view that the principle of utility is the correct principle for the society's public conception of justice' (TJ, p. 182). This is an excessively strict, and slightly idiosyncratic, view of what utilitarianism as a political philosophy is. It is also a potential source of confusion, inviting a conflation of two questions: that of what the criterion of justice is, and that of which charter is selected as just by the criterion. Be that as it may, however, Rawls's transcription of criteria as charters gives him, apart from the two-principles scheme, a charter which he describes simply as the principle of utility, and other charters corresponding to intuitionistic criteria of justice (TJ, p. 124). These make up a distinctive category among the alternative schemes with which the POP's are presented.

And what of the two-principles charter itself? This we must understand before we can grasp the other category of alternatives contemplated by Rawls: the variations on his preferred scheme. The two principles are: first, 'Each person is to have an equal right to the most extensive total system of equal basic liberties compatible with a similar system of liberty for all' (TJ, p. 250), and second, 'Social and economic inequalities are to be arranged so that they are both (a) to the greatest benefit of the least advantaged and (b) attached to offices and positions open to all under conditions of fair equality of opportunity' (TJ, p. 83; for a later reading, designed to cover intergenerational issues, see TJ, p. 302). The charter consists of these principles of social organisation combined with two important priority rules (TJ, pp. 302–3). The primary rule is that under normal non-starvation conditions the first principle should never be compromised in the name of the second: its lesser fulfilment is never justified by the greater satisfaction of the second principle; more intuitively, no interference with the system of liberties, whether in respect of extensiveness or equality, is compensated for by an increase in the socio-economic advantage of the society. The secondary rule of priority is mainly concerned with the relationship between the two parts of the second principle, ordaining that fair equality of opportunity should never be restricted out of consideration for

162

the greatest benefit of the least advantaged. The principles, together with the priority rules, make a sketchy but reasonably intelligible picture of how society might be organised and in particular they describe the system espoused by Rawls.

The category of political alternatives comprising variations on the two-principles charter is easily characterised. One variation mentioned by Rawls is a charter which combines the first principle with the principle of utility, this taking the place of the second principle given above, and others may be indefinitely imagined by the introduction of similar transformations (TJ, p. 124). One particularly interesting class of variations are described by Rawls as variant interpretations of the original formula. We get such interpretations for example as we alter the clauses in the second principle, replacing 'to the greatest benefit of the least advantaged' (the so-called difference principle) with 'to everyone's advantage' (the principle of efficiency) or removing 'fair equality of opportunity', as Nozick might want to do, in favour of 'careers open to talents' (TJ, pp. 65–75).

How then does Rawls's argument go for the superiority of the two-principles charter over the alternatives which he describes? Well, so far as the variations on the two principles go, he seems to take it without question that a POP who is of a maximinning bent will opt for the original formula. This is not an implausible supposition since the two principles, and in particular the second, look specifically to the welfare of the worst off person and are bound to keep the lowest position within the system higher than the corresponding station in the system organised by any variant. Rawls appears to make a similar assumption in respect of alternative charters which transcribe intuitionistic criteria, for the only argument that he mounts against competitors to the two-principles charter is addressed to the transcription of the utilitarian criterion. He urges that where the maximisation of utility may mean that some people do quite badly, and this point scarcely needs elaboration, the two principles guard against any such immiseration. Furthermore, he suggests that the extra benefits purchased for some individuals under the principle of utility charter are not likely to seem so very fantastic beside the solid values ensured under the two principles. Thus he presents the relationship between his preferred charter and the principle of utility as one which both ensures that the two principles are the maximin solution and, by the first two reasons given above for maximinning, guarantees that their adoption will seem incontestably rational. 'Any further advantages that might be won by the principle of utility, or whatever, are highly problematical, whereas the hardship if things turn out badly is intolerable' (TJ, p 175: 'is', the second last word, replaces 'are', an obvious slip in Rawls's text).

Rawls's argument for his two principles, as against the principle of utility, is supported by some detailed reasoning and it may be useful to summarise the considerations involved: these, it should be noticed, seek to establish only the maximin nature of the choice of the two principles; they do not bear out the stronger claim just mentioned. Three considerations are given in all (TJ, pp. 175–83). The first is that the POP runs the risk of having to take on a near impossible burden of commitment in voting for the principle of utility, whereas that burden is bound to be tolerable in any position under the two principles.

> In this respect the two principles of justice have a definite advantage. Not only do the parties protect their basic rights but they insure themselves against the worst eventualities. They run no chance of having to acquiesce in a loss of freedom over the course of their life for the sake of a greater good enjoyed by others, an undertaking that in actual circumstances they might not be able to keep.
> (TJ, p. 176)

The second consideration invoked by Rawls as a reason why a POP would prefer the two principles to the principle of utility is that even from within the original position it should be clear that the two-principles charter promises to be a more stable regime. A person living under that charter will feel satisfied that his own good is guaranteed and will naturally give the system his support. 'We can explain the acceptance of the social system and the principles it satisfies by the psychological law that persons tend to love, cherish, and support whatever affirms their own good' (TJ, p. 177). By contrast, someone living under the principle of utility charter may be disconsolate at his relative deprivation and will be required to rejoice in the welfare of others if he is to remain attached to the regime. The utilitarian charter must therefore be a more fragile construction. 'The principle of utility seems to require a greater identification with the interests of others than the two principles of justice. Thus the latter will be a more stable conception to the extent that this identification is difficult to achieve' (TJ, p. 177).

The third reason which Rawls gives why the maximin thing to prefer in the original position would be the two principles, rather than the principle of utility, relates closely to the second. It is that whereas the two principles guarantee a person's self-respect, the principle of utility puts it in jeopardy. 'When society follows these principles,' Rawls claims, 'everyone's good is included in a scheme of mutual benefit and this public affirmation in institutions of each man's endeavours supports men's self-esteem' (TJ, p. 179). By contrast he argues that when the principle of utility is used to organise society, a person may find that his prospects are belittled for the sake of a benefit to others, and that the basis of his self-respect is therefore threatened. 'Surely it is natural to experience a loss of self-esteem, a weakening of our sense of the value of accomplishing our aims, when we must accept a lesser prospect of life for the sake of others' (TJ, p. 181).

This, then, gives us a picture of Rawls's case for thinking that the maximin solution in the original position is, not the principle of utility, but his own two principles of justice. In conclusion I would like to draw attention to a more intuitive account which he offers elsewhere in *A Theory of Justice* of the reasoning which might lead the POP's to adopt the two principles, a train of reasoning that is only implicitly of a maximin nature. The account smacks less of casuistry than the case just summarised and it may have greater persuasive force.

According to the intuitive story we can imagine the POP's going through three stages of deliberation, in the last of which they espouse the two principles. At the first stage each POP reasons that the system which he should go for is naturally one that will guarantee the best that he can expect: an equal share with others in all social goods.

> There is no way for him to win special advantages for himself. Nor, on the other hand, are there grounds for his acquiescing in special disadvantages. Since it is not reasonable for him to expect more than an equal share in the division of social goods, and since it is not rational for him to agree to less, the sensible thing for him to do is to acknowledge as the first principle of justice one requiring an equal distribution. (TJ, p. 150)

At a second stage, however, the POP takes thought. It strikes him that the position of someone in an egalitarian system might be improved, were certain inequalities to be tolerated: the inequalities might serve as incentives to effort and might have a positive net effect. 'If there are inequalities in the basic structure that work to make everyone better off in comparison with the benchmark of initial equality, why not permit them?' (TJ, p. 151). The query has an irresistible effect, especially for someone untroubled by envy, and it leads the POP to adopt in place of an egalitarian charter, a principle of the following sort. 'All social values – liberty and opportunity, income and wealth, and the bases of self-respect – are to be distributed equally unless an unequal distribution of any, or all, of these values is to everyone's advantage' (TJ, p. 62).

The third stage of deliberation takes the POP's from this general conception of the just social arrangement to the special version of it enshrined in Rawls's two principles. The main cue for this further move is the recognition that there are some social values in which it would be irrational of someone to forgo an equal share for the sake of a greater helping of some other good: specifically, that it would be irrational to give up one's equal liberty in order to get greater social or economic advantage.

> This general conception imposes no constraints on what sorts of inequalities are allowed, whereas the special conception, by putting the two principles in serial order (with the necessary adjustments in meaning) forbids exchanges between basic liberties and economic and social benefits. . . . The idea underlying this ordering is that if the parties assume that their basic liberties can be effectively exercised, they will not exchange a lesser liberty for an improvement in economic well-being. (TJ, pp. 151–2)

This completes our presentation of the employment to which Rawls puts his contractarian criterion of justice. We took the original position as it was described in the last chapter and we asked two questions: one, what strategy of choice would be followed by the POP's; and two, what system would this strategy lead them to adopt. In discussing the first we saw that there were two serious candidates for consideration: the pessimist's strategy of maximinning, and the gambler's of maximising expected utility. Rawls argues for the maximinning procedure and we reviewed three reasons which he offers for thinking that this indeed would be the rational strategy for the POP's to adopt. Two of these have to do with the precise relationship between the alternatives on offer, the third bears on the difficulty of estimating probabilities from within the original position. We gave some time to the consideration of this third reason and we saw that Rawls drops a thick veil of ignorance over the original position rather than the thin one that would equally have served to eliminate the effects of bias and self-interest. In our discussion of the second question, the issue of what the maximin solution would be for someone in the original position, we described the alternatives considered by Rawls: the two-principles charter, some variations on that charter, and the transcriptions as charters of some traditional criteria of justice. We mentioned that he seemed to take it for granted, except in the case of the charter consisting in the principle of utility, that the two principles represented the maximin solution. We looked at the argument which he develops to cover the utilitarian alternative explicitly and we concluded with an informal account which he suggests in passing of the train of reasoning that the POP's might follow.

Bibliographical note

On all matters in the chapter the most importance source is *A Theory of Justice*, Oxford University Press, 1972. There is a useful introductory discussion of choice under uncertainty in Anthony Heath, *Rational Choice and Social Exchange*, Cambridge University Press, 1976. See also Richard Jeffrey, *The Logic of Decision*, McGraw-Hill, New York, 1965. A distinction between a thin and thick veil of ignorance is mentioned in R. M. Hare, 'Rawls's Theory of Justice', in Norman Daniels, ed., *Reading Rawls*, Blackwell, Oxford, 1975: what he has in mind, however, is not the precise distinction drawn by us. For a sophisticated discussion of different kinds of veils of ignorance see Isaac Levi, 'Four Types of Ignorance', *Social Research*, vol. 44, 1977.

16 Fairness under review

As we have seen in discussing the proprietarian and utilitarian criteria, there are three headings under which any proposed measure of justice calls to be examined. They are: the internal organisation of the criterion; its operation in the ranking of social schemes; and its normative output, i.e. the sort of arrangement which it tends to recommend. In this final chapter I propose to review the contractarian criterion on these counts, in order to determine how seriously it ought to be taken as an expression of the demands of social justice. Since the publication of *A Theory of Justice* just under a decade ago there have been numerous assessments of Rawls's work, including two full-length books and a collection of papers. My comments in what follows are influenced by this body of literature, though only in the measure allowed by my limited sympathy and modest erudition. They are not meant, however, to represent even a selection from the large span of criticisms encompassed in that literature. The task of sorting and sifting those criticisms must be left to another author; perhaps it will be taken up by Rawls in a second edition of his fine book.

On the matter of organisation there are two questions which I wish to consider in relation to the fairness criterion. The first has to do with whether there is anything to recommend the criterion intuitively, whether the idea that the just charter is that which would be chosen in the original position is unsurprising. It will be recalled from our discussion of the method of political philosophy in chapter 4 that a criterion is primarily designed to achieve reflective equilibrium with our intuitive judgments on more or less particular matters of justice: the success of the contractarian criterion in this respect will be considered under the heading of normative output. Any criterion, however, will be the more convincing for also satisfying certain general intuitions about the nature of justice and the considerations likely to determine it. After all, if a quite outlandish criterion happened to satisfy the test of reflective equilibrium we would still be loath to consider it a reconstruction of our sense of justice. The point is recognised by Rawls himself, for his emphasis on the importance of achieving reflective equilibrium in regard to the consequences of a criterion of justice is made in the context of recognising the desirability of fulfilling the other constraint. Thus he writes: 'the soundness of the theory of justice is shown as much in its consequences as in the prima facie acceptability of its premises' (TJ, p. 95).

Should we find unsurprising the idea that the charter chosen by the parties in the original position is the just arrangement of social affairs? Many commentators have thought so and in pressing the point they have variously emphasised the narrow sense in which the POP's are rational, their exclusive concern with their own interests, and the stultifying ignorance under which they labour. This is scarcely fair criticism, however, for there surely is something plausible in the general idea that a charter chosen by people in a situation that eliminates the effects of bias and self-interest is a just charter. Rawls insists on this aspect of his enterprise.

> The aim is to characterise this situation so that the
> principles that would be chosen, whatever they turn out to
> be, are acceptable from a moral point of view. The
> original position is defined in such a way that it is a status
> quo in which any agreements reached are fair. It is a state
> of affairs in which the parties are equally represented as
> moral persons and the outcome is not conditioned by
> arbitrary contingencies or the relative balance of social
> forces. (TJ, p. 120)

At the source of Rawls's contractarian approach is a powerful egalitarian intuition, as Ronald Dworkin has stressed. The original position is an appealing device for filtering out the requirements of justice because it is a decision procedure in which the equality of people is given institutional expression. What it lifts out is the charter which we, were we forced to respect one another's equality, would choose. Against this it has recently been suggested that the device deals only in ciphers: decision-makers whose essence is wholly contained in Rawls's specification of them as rational, mutually disinterested POP's. The idea is that it does not tell us what we, were we in the original position, would choose, on the grounds that if that were what it was telling us then questions such as the following would at least be sensible: 'Might we not get frustrated with the decision problem and end up sulking at one another?', 'Might we not refuse to go through the required deliberations?', 'Might we not just fall asleep?'. This objection is ill-conceived, for it may well be argued on behalf of Rawls that to go through with a piece of speculation which entertained questions like these would be practically impossible, and that the only way of getting at what we would choose in the original position is to find out what certain cipher surrogates would select in that situation.

But if we agree that there is something satisfyingly intuitive in the idea of the original position, we must still ask whether Rawls's specification of it is justified. This is the second question that I want to raise in regard to the organisation of the contractarian criterion. There are many aspects of Rawls's account of the original position to which it might be addressed but I will consider it only in relation to his specification of the primary goods. The point at issue is whether or not Rawls succeeds in giving a convincing picture of the original position, and the parties who exercise choice there; the background suspicion is that the picture is merely a projection of culture-bound prejudice.

It will be recalled that for Rawls the primary goods are things that the POP's desire as conditions the fulfilment of which is necessary if they are going to be able to satisfy whatever individually variable goals they turn out to have. The conditions are certain rights and liberties, opportunities and powers, income and wealth, and self-respect (TJ, p. 92). Does Rawls do anything to establish that these things are indeed primary goods? Well, he certainly sets out a strategy for arguing that they are. The items on his list are meant to be the goods to which the POP's are directed by certain general facts about human beings (TJ, p. 424). These include facts about human desires and wants, capacities and abilities, and social interdependence, but such matters are not discussed, on the ground that they are items of common sense knowledge (TJ, p. 425). The only relevant matter that is examined is something described as a deep psychological fact (TJ, p. 432). 'It says only that we prefer, other things equal, activities that depend upon a larger repertoire of realised capacities and that are more complex' (TJ, pp. 429–30). Rawls calls it the Aristotelian principle.

Rawls suggests that from the general facts at which he gestures the parties in the original position should be able to work out the primary goods and thus should be able to get their calculations going. Unfortunately, however, he does very little to give the suggestion argumentative weight. At the point where we might have expected the required deduction we are treated to a rather disappointing invocation of self-evidence.

We must assume, then, that the list of primary goods can
be accounted for by the conception of goodness as
rationality in connection with the general facts about
human wants and abilities, their characteristic phases and
requirements of nurture, the Aristotelian principle, and the
necessities of social interdependence. . I shall not argue
the case for the list of primary goods here, since their
claims seem evident enough. (TJ, p. 434)

The absence of a deduction of the primary goods raises a natural
doubt in the mind of a reader. Perhaps the conditions that appear
on Rawls's list are regarded as natural goals, both by him and by
us, only because of our habituation in a certain contemporary
style of life. Rawls appeals rather blandly to facts that are meant
to hold of people in all cultures and he assumes as a matter of
course that there are general psychological principles (TJ, pp. 24,
456), which include unspecified laws of motivation (TJ, p. 26).
We may reasonably complain about his suppositions in this
respect. There is serious question about the existence of universal
facts and principles such as he invokes and we may well suspect
that the mention of them merely conceals his parochialism.
Nothing has been said to still the feeling that the POP's have been
ascribed a locally specific mentality.

But it is unfair to say that Rawls offers no argument for his list
of primary goods. He does make a case out for the necessity of
one item on his list, self-respect. This he defines as (a) having a
sense of the value of one's plan in life and (b) having confidence
in one's ability to carry it out. He appeals to intuition in defence
of the idea that it ranks as a primary good. 'Without it nothing
may seem worth doing, or if some things have value for us, we
lack the will to strive for them' (TJ, p. 440). But here, as much
as in the cases where no argument is provided, the thought is
irresistible that Rawls is allowing himself to be carried away
uncritically by his own historically local experience, and that he
is not isolating something that inevitably matters to human beings.
He writes: 'what is necessary is that there should be for each
person at least one community of shared interests to which he
belongs and where he finds his endeavours confirmed by his associates' (TJ, p. 442, see also pp. 178–9). Is this something that
necessarily holds for people of all cultures, even for those who
are raised to put more importance than contemporary western
society does on the tradition or nation or church to which the
individual belongs? Perhaps it is; but perhaps again, it is not.

How are we to judge the question that is raised against Rawls?
Well we can reasonably complain that little is done to assure us

that the primary goods really are what they claim to be, and not just the projections of an anthropologically narrow imagination. But should the complaint be pressed further? Can one argue that the whole idea of the original position is undermined by the alleged relativity to culture of the things that people desire? I think not. If desires really are culture-bound in the suggested sense then all that the people of any culture can be interested in is the decision that their kind would make in the original position, and in this case there can be no objection to the postulation of primary goods that are locally distinctive. It is only because of the possibility that there are persuasive candidates for the role of universal primary goods that we can really complain at Rawls's easy appeals to common sense and psychology and at his lack of argument for the list of primary goods that he puts forward.

It appears then that while the original position device does have an undoubted intuitive appeal, we may at least complain against Rawls that he is less than his usual conscientious self in justifying his account of it, in particular his version of the primary goods which persons in the original position are said to pursue. So much by way of comment on the organisation of the contractarian criterion. We now have to submit the criterion to some questioning in regard to its mode of operation. Here again there are two queries that I wish to raise. First, is Rawls's argument for the maximin strategy convincing? And second, does he establish that maximinning would lead the POP's to choose the two principles?

It will be recalled that Rawls's first two arguments for the rationality of maximinning in the original position bore on the relation between the options presented. They were: that the best promised by alternatives to the two principles charter is not of significantly greater value than the worst guaranteed by that arrangement, and that the worst that such alternatives allow is downright intolerable. If such conditions are fulfilled then certainly we must say that the choice of the two principles, a maximin strategy, is the uniquely rational one. As we saw, Rawls believes that at least so far as the utilitarian alternative goes the conditions are indeed satisfied. However, he does not set out to prove this explicitly, the reasons which he develops for the choice of the two principles having to do only with the maximin nature of that choice.

But in any case Rawls's specification of alternatives to the two principles is scarcely rich enough for us to be impressed by the claim that his preferred charter meets such powerful constraints. The list is restricted to some variations on the two principles, and some traditional conceptions of the just society. And it is further marred by the fact that in considering a traditional conception such as the utilitarian charter, Rawls takes this to mean: not that charter, whatever it is, which promises to secure maximum happiness; but rather the charter which is fully characterised in the injunction to maximise happiness. This representation of the utilitarian's ideal society seems scarcely charitable, especially when one considers that the charter is expected to meet the constraints of right, and in particular that it is to be the publicly recognised means of resolving any issues that come up. The utilitarian system envisaged by Rawls is a brave new world in which the solutions to political issues are constantly adjusted and amended as new information comes in on the state of want-satisfaction in the community. This is not necessarily the charter which a utilitarian would prefer; it is the charter that would obtain were the legal authorities practising utilitarians, something that the utilitarian philosopher might wish they were not.

Rawls offers only one argument for maximinning that is independent of the alternatives presented in the original position, and that is unaffected therefore by the inadequacy of his list of alternatives. This is the argument from the unavailability of the probability figures required if the POP's are to consider maximising expected utility rather than maximinning. Unfortunately, however, this piece of reasoning is not very persuasive in view of the fact that such figures would be available under a thin veil of ignorance, and a thin veil would serve the contractarian purpose of eliminating the effects of self-interest and bias. As we saw, Rawls opts for a thick veil, but he does nothing to justify this option; indeed he scarcely shows any awareness of the possibility of construing the veil of ignorance otherwise than he does. Under the thin veil the POP's suppose that they will be accorded their respective social positions in the system chosen, by a process of random distribution; under the thick they take it that they will accede to such positions in accordance with their talent, effort and fortune. The thin veil would allow the POP's to reason that they each have the same chance of being in any given social station, the thick would force them to recognise that their chances vary, although in an unknown pattern. Rawls does nothing to establish that the original position makes probability calculations impossible because he gives no reason for thinking that a thick rather than a thin veil ought to be dropped over that situation of choice.

It seems then that Rawls fails to make his case for the maximinning strategy. His argument from the unavailability of probabilities looks to be a dead-end, and his arguments from the nature of the alternatives need to be backed by a more careful account of the options between which the POP's have to choose.

Our second question in regard to the operation of the contractarian criterion has to do with whether maximinning would in any case lead to the choice of the two principles but before we take that up we may just mention the likely reason why Rawls is anxious to make a case for the maximin strategy. It is that if the POP's maximise expected utility in their choice of system then there is every reason to believe that what they choose will coincide with the preference of the unreformed utilitarian. In particular they will not necessarily shrink from a charter that does badly by a minority, since the gambling value of that system may yet be very high. But in that case the contractarian criterion will fall foul of reflective equilibrium in just the way that utilitarianism does: it will fail to guard against inequalities that we intuitively find intolerable. If contractarianism is to sail by those rocks on which the welfare criterion flounders it is vital that the parties in the original position be taken to behave like pessimists rather than gamblers.

It may be that maximinning can be justified in a fuller consideration of the options put before the POP's, or on some grounds not mentioned by Rawls. Where then would maximinning lead the parties? Would it necessarily support the choice of the two principles, as Rawls maintains? This question, like the preceding one, is impossible to judge with any confidence in the absence of a thoroughly worked out list of the alternative charters with which the POP's are presented. My own feeling is that something like the two principles would indeed be selected but I do not intend to try to justify this other than by reminding the reader of the sorts of grounds that Rawls quotes in his case against utilitarianism, and in his intuitive account of the reasoning that the POP's might go through.

However, there is one unexamined assumption in Rawls's work which threatens his argument that the two principles are the maximin solution and we may usefully draw attention to this. Rawls supposes that each party in the original position compares the worst off positions within the different systems presented to him, and ranks them ordinally for the extent to which they satisfy primary goods (TJ, pp. 91–2). The crucial element in this supposition is the idea that each person will want more rather than less of the goods in question.

> Regardless of what an individual's rational plans are in
> detail, it is assumed that there are various things which he
> would prefer more of rather than less. With more of these
> goods men can generally be assured of greater success in
> carrying out their intentions and in advancing their ends,

whatever these ends may be. (TJ, p. 92, see also pp. 396–7)

But as Brian Barry has pointed out, an individual may not want the greatest liberty or wealth available to him if the circumstances under which he gets this are ones where everyone else has a similar abundance: when the abundance is collective, the situation may radically change, as will be clear from a moment's reflection on the characteristics of the extremely libertarian or affluent society. It would seem then that in maximinning the POP will not necessarily go for the system whose worst off position gives maximal satisfaction of the primary goods on Rawls's list. These goods may be wanted in maximum supply, only under the condition that certain social patterns are realised. The appropriate sort of constraint needs to be written into the list of primary goods before we can be sure where maximinning would lead the parties in the original position. Thus we return to the point of criticism made in relation to the organisation of the contractarian criterion, that Rawls does not pay sufficient attention to the justification of his list of primary goods.

So far our criticisms of the contractarian approach can be read, not as deeply subversive comments, but only as complaints that Rawls, however heroic his efforts, has not done important parts of his job well enough: in particular that he has not devoted enough care either to the construction of the list of primary goods or to the devising of the list of alternatives with which the parties in the original position are presented. We come finally to the crucial count on which a criterion of justice has to be assessed: that of whether its normative output is satisfactory, the recommendations that it supports being in reflective equilibrium with our intuitive judgments of justice. Assuming that the contractarian criterion does support the two principles as the just charter for the organisation of society, does this mean that the criterion passes the test of reflective equilibrium?

In dealing with the proprietarian and utilitarian criteria of justice we did not consider in any detail the regimes that they supported. We did not really need to do so because in each case we found a feature likely to appear in the sort of dispensation supported which was intuitively intolerable, or which at any rate seemed to be intolerable within this individual's habits of judgment. It turned out that proprietarianism would justify a certain pattern of inherited privilege and deprivation and that utilitarianism would give its blessing to certain sorts of inequality. Is there any single feature in the two principles charter which looks to be equally objectionable, and which might save us the job of considering the detailed ramifications of the arrangement?

The most direct challenge that has been made to Rawls's charter, and it applies to any regime that imposes a structural ideal of distribution, is that which comes from Nozick, to the effect that such an arrangement is indistinguishable from slavery. It will be recalled from chapter ten that Nozick tells the tale of a slave whose lot is gradually improved, until the slave finds himself in much the position of a citizen in a redistributive state, and that he then challenges the reader to give reason for drawing the line between slavery and non-slavery somewhere along the continuum of improvements. Against Nozick's challenge, however, we made the point that whether or not one finds reason for drawing such a line depends precisely on one's background philosophy and that someone of a redistributivist outlook will have no difficulty in justifying the appropriate demarcation to himself.

Does any equally central challenge to the two principles have some plausibility? Well, Rawls might be accused of endorsing a curiously rigid dispensation in arguing that no amount of socioeconomic advantage would compensate for a diminution in the most extensive system of equal liberties, especially since these liberties are not particularly restricted: they include political freedom, freedom of thought, speech and assembly, freedom of person and (personal) property, and freedom from arbitrary arrest (TJ, p. 61), but apparently they also extend to such privileges as 'the important liberty of free choice of occupation' (TJ, p. 274). Any assault on this count, however, is likely to be parried by the open-ended qualification which Rawls puts on the priority of liberty, that if a society is not sufficiently well-off to ensure the effective realisation of equal liberties, then liberty may be traded for socio-economic advantage (TJ, p. 152). No society that I know of has been able effectively to realise the equal liberty of people to choose their occupations and at least in respect of that freedom then the priority rule would not seem to apply. It is not clear how widely Rawls means to use the qualification: as we have seen, he stipulates rather strictly that the circumstances for which the POP's are choosing a social charter do admit of the effective realisation of equal liberties. However, one suspects that if pressure is put on the two principles arrangement for its consecration and indeed idolisation of liberty, the qualification can always be invoked to stave off criticism.

There is a second point at which the two principles may also seem to be open to fairly basic challenge but here again Rawls proves to be something of a moving target. It may be said that the principles pay absurd attention to the position of the worst off person, and that they have the following intolerable results: that so long as the worst off are at the same level the principles would be indifferent between two systems in one of which people other than the worst off are much better treated than they are in the other, and that so long as it improved by a tittle the position of the worst off person, the principles would prefer a system that greatly impaired the lot of those other than the worst off. Rawls's general response to these difficulties is to say that they are empirically unlikely, in view of the connections between the welfare levels of different positions in a society (TJ, pp. 80–3). This rebuttal makes for an effective stalemate, since the empirical question is not one that allows of easy resolution. It may be mentioned that the second is the more pressing problem since, as Rawls notices, he is free to respond to the first with an amendment to the second principle, suggested by Amartya Sen (TJ, p. 83). This amendment would replace the simple difference principle with an ordered one: a principle that would rank systems initially by the welfare of the worst off positions, as in the simple case, but which would break the tie between two equally ranked systems by the welfare of the second worst off positions, and so on up the hierarchy until all ties are settled.

The lesson to be learned from these tentative assaults on Rawls's two principles is surely that, unlike the charters recommended by the rival criteria of justice, the charter which these comprise is not in flagrant conflict with our native intuitions as to how political issues ought to be resolved. If the dispensation fails the test of reflective equilibrium then it does not do so in any obvious way. At this point the task which lies before the political philosopher is to follow Rawls in explicating the exact content of the two principles and in expanding on their implementation. What he has to judge is whether the consequences of the contractarian criterion, as they are brought to light in this process, achieve the desired degree of equilibrium with his considered judgments on the demands of justice. The task however is an enormous one and we shall surely be pardoned if we set it to one side. Our policy has been to concern ourselves primarily with the rival criteria of justice and to avoid getting entangled in the detail of the charters that they recommend. This would be an unhappy point to break with it, for doing so would mean that we were in the middle of our ruminations on theories of justice, instead of at a stage where we can begin to draw them to a close.

In this chapter we set out to examine the contractarian criterion on the usual scores of organisation, operation and output. We found under the heading of organisation that the criterion is an intuitively compelling one but that the specification of the original position, particularly in the identification of primary goods, requires more careful handling than that which Rawls gives it. Under the title of operation we urged that both the argument for maximinning and the argument for the two principles suffer from the inadequate account provided of the alternatives with which the POP's are presented. We also saw that, as Brian Barry has emphasised, Rawls is rash to assume that the parties will always be concerned to maximise the payoff accruing to them in primary goods: this gave us another reason for thinking that greater care is needed in the specification of those goods. Finally, we argued that the two principles, if indeed they are the output most naturally forthcoming from the contractarian criterion, have the conspicuous merit of not offending against our intuitions on justice in a flagrant manner. The brunt of these criticisms then is that while contractarianism may not be up and kicking, it cannot be laid to rest in the fashion in which we despatched its proprietarian and (unmodified) utilitarian competitors. There is life in the young dog yet.

Bibliographical note

The two books on Rawls's work are Brian Barry, *The Liberal Theory of Justice*, Oxford University Press, 1973, and Robert Paul Wolff, *Understanding Rawls*, Princeton University Press, 1977. The collection of papers dealing with his work is Norman Daniels, ed., *Reading Rawls*, Blackwell, Oxford, 1975. The egalitarian aspect of the original position device is discussed by Ronald Dworkin in 'The Original Position', reprinted in Daniels and, as chapter 6, in *Taking Rights Seriously*, Duckworth, London, 1978: as with utilitarianism, Dworkin argues that whatever force the criterion has derives from its claim to treat individuals as equals. The criticism that the original position is a possible world which reveals how cipher decision-makers would vote, and not concrete people, is developed in Micahel E. Levin and Margarita Levin, 'The Modal Confusion in Rawls's Original Position', in *Analysis*, vol. 39, 1979. The culture-bound aspect of Rawls's theory, including that of his account of primary goods, is pursued in my article 'A Theory of Justice?' in *Theory and Decision*, vol. 4, 1974. A veil of ignorance technique which is assumed to make the parties maximise expected utility was developed in 1953 by John C. Harsanyi. See his 'Cardinal Utility in Welfare Economics and in the Theory of Risk-Taking', reprinted in *Essays on Ethics, Social Behaviour and Scientific Explanation*, Reidel, Dordrecht, 1976. Brian Barry's criticism of Rawls for missing the effect of collective abundance on an individual's desire for a particular good is presented in chapter 11 of *The Liberal Theory of Justice*. The priority of liberty is discussed in a number of papers in Daniels: see in particular H. L. A. Hart, 'Rawls on Liberty and its Priority'. The ordered difference principle is suggested in Amartya Sen, *Collective Choice and Social Welfare*, Oliver & Boyd, London, 1970, chapter 9.

Conclusion

Political philosophy, by the account developed in Part I, is the attempt to spell out what social justice means: to offer a criterion for the just resolution of political issues, and ultimately for the selection of the ideal political charter. More specifically, as we came to see in Part II, it is the attempt to say how the organisation of society, the alignment between the legal, the economic and the civil aspects of social life, can be best made to answer to the interests of individuals. The different philosophies that we have examined offer competing interpretations of what it is for those interests to be institutionally respected. Proprietarianism takes the satisfaction of interests to lie in the recognition of natural rights, utilitarianism in the maximisation of utilities, and contractarianism in the fulfilment of enlightened preferences.

The argument of the last three parts of the text has tended to the conclusion that justice cannot be satisfactorily measured by a yardstick of rights or utilities, and that there are difficulties with the standard which enlightened preferences give us. The upshot is not very exciting but neither is it gloomy: contractarianism, and indeed the modified utilitarianism in which it is adumbrated, offers a straightforward criterion of justice which we have not found conclusive reason for rejecting. It may well be that in this doctrine, or in some descendant of it, there will be crystallised an understanding of justice which will meet all the constraints that we could wish to impose and which will attract an overwhelming consensus of reasoned opinion.

But if we do not allow ourselves to indulge in such a prospect, we must want to ask if it at least appears, at the end of our investigation, that political philosophy has got a future. Is the project buoyant and on course, or does it seem that sooner or later it must run aground? Even when we put aside the institutionalist claims which would altogether undermine the enterprise, we find ourselves faced by various counsels of pessimism. As we saw in chapter 3, the intuitionist would deny that any fully articulated criterion can capture our intuitions about justice, while the conservative and the consensualist would offer a more radically sceptical challenge, denying to us the freedom from ideology which would be required for objective political assessment.

Against the intuitionist challenge it can be said that what we have seen gives us reason to think that there is as bright a prospect for completely defined criteria of justice as there is for criteria which leave crucial matters of weighting to intuitive discretion. The failures which we found in the philosophies examined are not of a kind which would have us look more optimistically to intuitionistic interpretations of the demands of justice.

But what are we to say to the more radical sceptical challenge? This, especially in the form in which it does not suppose institutionalism, comes usually from a Marxist point of view. The claim is made that the sort of thinking involved in political philosophy is bourgeois or ideological, undialectical or unhistorical: a paradigm of false consciousness. This claim is in turn based on a theory of social formation, in particular a theory of the social formation of ideas.

Perhaps the first thing to be said to the Marxist is that he is scarcely in a position himself to disavow all concern with justice, in view of his involvement in criticism of existing social structure: the comment is *ad hominem,* but it reveals just how deeply the sceptical challenge would cut. If the demands of justice are not something that we can sensibly think of construing in an objective manner, then what is it that vindicates the Marxist critique of capitalist society? It will not do for the Marxist to invoke the march of history, for the fact that present structures are doomed, if indeed they are so, does nothing to show that their demise should be applauded or hastened.

There have been many responses within Marxism to this problem, none of them wholly successful. Alasdair MacIntyre makes the following comment.

Marx originally indicted capitalist values as well as
capitalist methods. His belief that any appeal to the
exploiters on a moral basis was bound to embody the
illusion of common standards of justice governing human
behaviour made him suspicious of all moralising. But when
Eduard Bernstein attempted to find a Kantian basis for
socialism, the defenders of Marxist orthodoxy Karl
Kautsky and Rosa Luxembourg were forced to reopen the
question of the nature of the moral authority of the

Marxist appeal to the working class. This question, as the experience of Luxembourg and of Lukacs, of Trotsky and of Guevara shows, was never satisfactorily answered.

Habermas's consensus theory of justice may be seen as a contemporary response to this problem. It identifies the just social order as that which would attract consensus under ideal conditions of debate and negotiation, conditions where people would sort out their real interests from their illusory ones, and their common interests from those that divide them. It denies, however, that we are in a position within the imperfect *status quo* to work out exactly what charter would command such rational consensus: the best we can attempt is a hazardous guess. The criterion is one which the Marxist critic may claim, with due diffidence, to be applying; he is gambling on what people would opt for in a rational consensus. However, it is not a criterion which can raise ideological worries, for by leaving us in an agnostic position about what scheme would satisfy the condition it defers appropriately to the constraints of social formation.

Habermas tries to have his cake and eat it. Elsewhere I have examined his arguments in detail and I have tried to show that generally they do not secure the agnostic result he desires. It thus appears that by committing himself on the criterion of justice, he cannot help but license the enterprise of applying that criterion and doing political philosophy, an enterprise which the Marxist theory of social formation would have him castigate. If this case against Habermas is successful, and if there is no other way for the Marxist to solve the problem that we posed, then it seems that our original *ad hominem* comment stands. There is no plausible way of securing a critical stance on the existing social order other than by endorsing the activity of political philosophy explored in this text. The thought should at least give pause to those who are radically sceptical about the investigation of the nature of justice.

But, in fairness, Habermas does point to one possibility that might legitimate his agnostic theory of justice. He suggests in some of his writing that many of the interests which a just charter would satisfy are not like biological needs: they are not naturally present in everyone, albeit under different cultural forms. The idea is that they are more of a piece with artistic needs, such as the need that one may develop for classical music: specifically, that they appear under appropriate conditions as if out of nowhere, not having been detectable beforehand. If such a theory of need-formation is allowed, and if the just dispensation is identified as that which best satisfies people's real needs, then it may indeed seem rash to try to work out in advance what arrangement would be chosen by people under conditions facilitating the appearance of such interests.

The student of justice must concern himself at this juncture with questions about the nature of human needs. Perhaps when such issues have been fully investigated it will be clearer whether the consensualist challenge can indeed be put aside. My own hope is that the challenge can be met, for my fear is that putting justice out of cognitive reach may mean inhibiting detailed social criticism, and indulging the romantic vision that someday everything will be changed, changed utterly. In the meantime the relatively mundane business of explicating the concept of justice goes on. As this book leaves the typewriter, yet a further approach to the concept has been outlined. Frederick Schick suggests in a forthcoming article that the proper understanding of justice might be not proprietarian, or utilitarian, or contractarian, but liberal: this, in the sense that the just society furthers people's resources, their control over their destinies, rather than satisfying their rights, maximising their utilities, or meeting their enlightened preferences. The proliferation of theories of justice can hardly be a bad sign: it suggests that whatever its ultimate destiny, the research programme of political philosophy will be with us for some time yet.

Bibliographical note

For a sobering account of the difficulties in our established political ideals see John Dunn, *Western Political Theory in the Face of the Future*, Cambridge University Press, 1979. Anthony Skillen, *Ruling Illusions*, Harvester, Brighton, 1977, mounts a stinging attack on what he sees as the tendency of academic philosophy, especially political philosophy, to leave the real causes of social misery unindicted. The quotation from MacIntyre is from pp. 92–3 of *Against the Self-Images of the Age*, Duckworth, London, 1971. My examination of Habermas is developed in 'Habermas on Truth and Justice', in G. H. R. Parkinson, *Marx and Marxisms*, Harvester, Brighton, forthcoming. The article by Frederick Schick is 'Towards a Logic of Liberalism', *Journal of Philosophy*, forthcoming.

Bibliography

Antaki, Charles, ed., *The Psychology of Ordinary Explanation*, Academic Press, London, forthcoming.

Arblaster, Anthony and Lukes, Steven, eds., *The Good Society*, Methuen, London, 1971.

Arrow, Kenneth, 'Values and Decision-Making', in Laslett and Runciman, 1967.

Barker, Ernest, ed., *The Social Contract*, Oxford University Press, 1947.

Barry, Brian, *Political Argument*, Routledge & Kegan Paul, London, 1965.

Barry, Brian, *The Liberal Theory of Justice*, Oxford University Press, 1973.

Becker, Lawrence, *Property Rights*, Routledge & Kegan Paul, London, 1977.

Bentham, Jeremy, *An Introduction to the Principles of Morals and Legislation*, Hafner, New York, 1970.

Blau, Peter, ed., *Social Structure*, Open Books, London, 1976.

Blom-Cooper, Louis and Drewry, Gavin, ed., *Law and Morality: A Reader*, Duckworth, London, 1976.

Bolton, Neil, ed., *Philosophical Problems in Psychology*, Methuen, London, 1979.

Bowie, N.E. and Simon, R. L., *The Individual and the Political Order*, Prentice-Hall, Englewood Cliffs, NJ, 1977.

Brand, Myles, ed., *The Nature of Causation*, University of Illinois Press, Urbana, 1976.

Braybrooke, David, *Three Tests for Democracy*, Random House, New York, 1968.

Coleman, James, 'Social Structure and the Theory of Action', in Blau, 1976.

Coleman, James, S., *Power and the Structure of Society*, Norton, New York, 1974.

Cranston, Maurice, *What are Human Rights?*, Bodley Head, London, 1973.

Crosland, Anthony, *The Future of Socialism*, Schocken, London, 1956.

Daniels, Norman, ed., *Reading Rawls*, Blackwell, Oxford, 1975.

Daniels, Norman, 'Wide Reflective Equilibrium and Theory Acceptance in Ethics', *Journal of Philosophy*, vol. 76, 1979.

Devlin, Patrick, *The Enforcement of Morals*, Oxford University Press, 1965.

Dunn, John., *Western Political Theory in the Face of the Future*, Cambridge University Press, 1979.

Dworkin, Ronald, *Taking Rights Seriously*, Duckworth, London, 1978.

Glover, Jonathan, *Causing Death and Saving Lives*, Penguin, Harmondsworth, 1975.

Goodman, Nelson, *Fact, Fiction and Forecast*, Bobbs-Merrill, New York, 3rd edn., 1973.

Hare, R. M., *The Language of Morals*, Oxford University Press, 1952.

Hare, R. M., *Freedom and Reason*, Oxford University Press, 1963.

Harrison, Ross, ed., *Rational Action*, Cambridge University Press, 1979.

Harsanyi, John C., *Essays on Ethics, Social Behaviour and Scientific Explanation*, Reidel, Dordrecht, 1976.

Hart, H. L. A., *The Concept of Law*, Oxford University Press, 1961.

Hart, H. L. A., *Law, Liberty and Morality*, Oxford University Press, 1962.

Hart, H. L. A., 'Rawls on Liberty and its Priority', in Daniels, 1975.

Hayek, F. A., 'Scientism and The Study of Society', in O'Neill, 1973.

Hayek, F. A., *Law, Legislation and Liberty*, vol. 2 *The Mirage of Social Justice*, Routledge & Kegan Paul, London, 1976.

Heath, Anthony, *Rational Choice and Social Exchange*, Cambridge University Press, 1976.

Hesse, Mary, 'Models of Theory Change', in Suppes *et al.,* 1973.

Hesse, Mary, *The Structure of Scientific Inference*, Macmillan, London, 1974.

Hobbes, Thomas, *Leviathan*, ed., C. B. McPherson, Allen Lane, Harmondsworth, 1968.

Honderich, Ted, *Punishment: The Supposed Justifications*, Penguin, Harmondsworth, 1971.

Hookway, Christopher and Pettit, Philip, eds., *Action and Interpretation*, Cambridge University Press, 1978.

Jeffrey, Richard, *The Logic of Decision*, McGraw-Hill, New York, 1965.

Jeffrey, Richard, 'On Interpersonal Utility Theory', *Journal of Philosophy*, vol. 68, 1971.

Kamenka, Eugene and Erh-Soon Tay, Alice, eds, *Human Rights*, Edward Arnold, London, 1978.

Laslett, Peter and Runciman, W. G., eds., *Philosophy, Politics and Society*, Cambridge University Press, 1967.

Levi, Isaac, 'Four Types of Ignorance', *Social Research*, vol. 44, 1977.

Levin, Michael, E. and Levin Margarita, 'The Modal Confusion in Rawls's Original Position', *Analysis*, vol. 39, 1979.

Lewis, David, *Convention*, Harvard University Press, 1969.

Lively, Jack, *Democracy*, Blackwell, Oxford, 1975.

Bibliography

Locke, John, *Two Treatises of Government*, ed. P. Laslett, Cambridge University Press, 1963.

Lukes, Steven, *Individualism*, Blackwell, Oxford, 1973.

Macdonald, Graham and Pettit, Philip, *Semantics and Social Science*, Routledge & Kegan Paul, London, forthcoming.

MacIntyre, Alasdair, *Against the Self Images of the Age*, Duckworth, London, 1971.

MacKenzie, Norman, *Socialism*, 2nd edn, Hutchinson, London, 1966.

Melden, A. I., ed., *Natural Rights*, Wadsworth, Belmont, California, 1970.

Mill, John Stuart, *Utilitarianism, Liberty and Representative Government*, Dent, London, 1972.

Miller, David, *Social Justice*, Oxford University Press, 1976.

Montefiore, Alan, *Philosophy and Personal Relations*, Routledge & Kegan Paul, London, 1973.

Nagel, Ernest, *The Structure of Science*, Routledge & Kegan Paul, London, 1961.

Nozick, Robert, *Anarchy, State and Utopia*, Blackwell, Oxford, 1974.

Oakeshott, Michael, *Rationalism in Politics*, Methuen, London, 1962.

O'Neill, John, ed., *Modes of Individualism and Collectivism*, Heinemann, London, 1973.

Parfit, Derek, 'Later Selves and Moral Principles', in Montefiore, 1973.

Parkinson, G. H. R., *Marx and Marxisms*, Harvester, Brighton, forthcoming.

Perry, R. B., *General Theory of Value*, Longmans Green, New York, 1926.

Pettit, Philip, 'A Theory of Justice', *Theory and Decision*, vol. 4., 1974.

Pettit, Philip, 'Review of Nozick 1974', *Theory and Decision*, vol. 8, 1977.

Pettit, Philip, 'Rational Man Theory', in Hookway and Pettit, 1978.

Pettit, Philip, 'Rationalisation and the Art of Explaining Action', in Bolton, 1979.

Pettit, Philip, 'Habermas on Truth and Justice', in Parkinson, forthcoming.

Plamenatz, John, *The English Utilitarians*, rev. edn, Blackwell, Oxford, 1958.

Quine, W. V. O., *From a Logical Point of View*, Harvard University Press, 1953.

Quinton, Anthony, *Utilitarian Ethics*, Macmillan, London, 1973.

Ramsey, Frank, *Foundations*, ed. D. H. Mellor, Routledge & Kegan Paul, London, 1978.

Rawls, John, *A Theory of Justice*, Oxford University Press, 1972.

Rawls, John, 'A Kantian Conception of Morality', *Cambridge Review*, vol. 96, no. 2225, 1975.

Rescher, Nicholas, *Distributive Justice*, Bobbs-Merrill, New York, 1966.

Richards, D. A. J., *A Theory of the Reasons for Action*, Oxford University Press, 1971.

Ritchie, D. G., *Natural Rights*, Allen & Unwin, London, 1894.

Robbins, Lionel, *An Essay on the Nature and Significance of Economic*

Science, Macmillan, London, 1932.

Ryan, Alan, *John Stuart Mill*, Routledge & Kegan Paul, London, 1974.

Sartre, J. P., *Being and Nothingness*, trans. H. Barnes, Methuen, London, 1957.

Schick, Frederic, 'Towards a Logic of Liberalism', *Journal of Philosophy*, forthcoming.

Sen, Amartya K., *Collective Choice and Social Welfare*, Oliver & Boyd, London, 1970.

Sen, Amartya K., 'Informational Analysis of Moral Principles', in Harrison, 1979.

Sidgwick, Henry, *The Methods of Ethics*, Macmillan, London, 1962.

Singer, Peter, 'Sidgwick and Reflective Equilibrium', *The Monist*, vol. 58, 1974.

Skillen, Anthony, *Ruling Illusions*, Harvester, Brighton, 1977.

Smart, J. J. C. and Williams, Bernard, *Utilitarianism: For and Against*, Cambridge University Press, 1973.

Suppes, Patrick, *et al., Logic, Methodology and Philosophy of Science*, Amsterdam, 1973.

Tuck, Richard, *Natural Rights Theories*, Cambridge University Press, 1979.

Ullman-Margalit, Edna, *The Emergence of Norms*, Oxford University Press, 1977.

Ullman-Margalit, Edna, 'Invisible Hand Explanations', *Synthese*, vol. 39, 1978.

Waldner, Ilmar, 'The Empirical Meaningfulness of Interpersonal Utility Comparisons', *Journal of Philosophy*, vol. 69, 1972.

Weale, Albert, *Equality and Social Policy*, Routledge & Kegan Paul, London, 1978.

Wiggins, David, 'Truth, Invention and the Meaning of Life', *Proceedings of the British Academy*, vol. 62, 1976.

Wolff, Robert Paul, *Understanding Rawls*, Princeton University Press, 1977.

Index of names

Index

Index of subjects

action, 55–6
anarchy, 6, 14, 85–6
authority, 4, 10–12
autonomy: explanatory, 52–3, 59–64; expressive, 50–2; ontological, 48–53

charter, 21, 24–5, 150–1; versus allocation, 99–100; versus criterion, 25, 161–2; *see also* two principles
collectivism, *see* institutionalism
comparison, interpersonal, 121, 124–5, 144
compensation, 81–2, 88–9, 97
consensualism, xi, 27–8, 30, 181–3
conservatism, 27–8, 30, 47, 181
contractarianism, ix–x, 29, 143, 147–55, 156–67, 168–79
criterion of justice, 25–30; evaluation of, 31–42, 94, 102–3, 129, 145, 168; as ground, not generalisation, 38, 96, 103, 168–9; other characterisations, 25–6; scalar, 26–7, 30; serial, 26, 30; singular, 28–30; *see also* charter

decision theory, 32, 35, 153, 157–62, 172–4; *see also* method; rationality
democracy, 11, 21–2; and demoktesis, 91–2
desire, 55–6, 112–13, 172

difference principle, 162–3, 177; *see also* two principles

efficiency principle, 163
envy, 153
equality, equal treatment and treatment as equal, 131–2
ethics, 32, 35, 110, 112, 115–17, 154
executive, 10
explanation, 52; invisible hand, 85–9, 93

fairness, x, 30, 101, 133–5, 143
foundationalism, 38
functionalism, 46, 53

group, 2, 3, 7–8, 45, 48–9, 60

happiness, 111–13, *see also* welfare
historicism, 46–7
holism, *see* institutionalism
humanism, 55–9, 63–4

impossibility theorem, Arrow's, 145–6
individualism, 65–6; ontological, x–xi, 45–53, 59–64, 65–71; developmental, 66–7; epistemological, 67; ethical, 69–70; heuristic, 68–9; methodological, 67–8; policy-making, 70–1; *see also* reformism
inquiry, reflective, 31–3, 35–9; empirical, 33–5